PLAN B

THE FUTURE OF THE REST OF CANADA

PLAN B

THE FUTURE OF THE REST OF CANADA

GORDON GIBSON

THE FRASER
INSTITUTE

The author of this book has worked independently and opinions expressed by him, therefore, are his own, and do not necessarily reflect the opinions of the members or the trustees of The Fraser Institute.

Printed in Canada.

Canadian Cataloguing in Publication Data

Gibson, Gordon, 1937-
Plan B

Includes bibliographical references.
ISBN 0-88975-170-6

   1. Quebec (Province)—History—Autonomy and independence movements. 2. Canada—English-French relations. 3. Canada—Politics and government   I. Fraser Institute (Vancouver, B.C.) II. Title.

FC2925.9S4G52 1994   971.4'04   C94-910550-3
F1027.G52 1994

Contents

Acknowledgements . . . . *vi*
About the author . . . . *viii*
Note to the Second Printing . . . . *ix*
Preface by Michael A. Walker . . . . *xi*
Dedication . . . . *xvi*

Chapter 1: Introduction—The need for a "Plan B" . . . **1**

Chapter 2: The Beginning—of the End? **9**

Chapter 3: First Things First—the Transition **33**

Chapter 4: The Major Questions for ROC **49**

Chapter 5: Attitudes **75**

Chapter 6: The Doughnut and Other Shapes **91**

Chapter 7: Bargaining with Quebec—
Machinery and Issues **109**

Chapter 8: Stuck Together or Disassembled—
Pieces of the ROC **131**

Chapter 9: Reprise and Stock-taking **179**

Chapter 10: "Plan C" **189**

Epilogue **209**

Appendix I: "Saying No"—Refusing to
Negotiate and UDI **211**

Acknowledgements

THE POTENTIAL NEED FOR A BOOK OF THIS KIND became apparent within a few months following the results of the October 1993 federal election. The political determination to pretend that the constitutional file was a non-issue was clearly not going to work. The decision to commission this work was made at the end of March 1994. Since time was clearly of the essence with a Quebec election on the immediate horizon, a writing deadline of June 1 was set, and met.

Much of what follows is new territory, and like all explorers, we will go down some dead-end valleys and meet impassable mountains or streams. But at the end, much of the new territory will have been mapped. If in the process we see something more, much is owed to previous explorers who stopped at the Quebec-ROC border—a phrase that will be clearer after a chapter or two. To those few, listed in footnotes throughout, a great debt is acknowledged.

In this book we go beyond that border and probe the shifting foundations of the rest of Canada, to see if they will hold or if we can shore them up. There has been much help along the way. First and foremost must be the staff of The Fraser Institute, in particular Isabella Horry and Gary Khangura who supplied in-depth economic backup, and Kristin McCahon and Scott Fromson, who copyedited and typeset the manuscript, all on unreasonably short request. Special gratitude is due to the Canada West Foundation, particularly David Elton and Peter McCormack, who were generous with facts and suggestions. And I have a great and lasting debt to my assistant of many years, Mary Murray.

Several other friends across the country were also good enough to read the manuscript and correct errors—most, it is hoped.

But this is a work in progress. As Michael Walker says in his preface, no new exploration of an imponderable future this vast, this important to millions of individuals' lives, can help but be improved by a thousand insights of those who have a grip on another corner of reality that will make a difference. Write your own books, or help us write the next edition of this future history of our country with your comments and advice.

This subject will be with us for some time to come. May this help. And may I give final acknowledgement to the person who got it started in a conversation with Michael Walker some three months ago. He knows who he is.

G.F.G.

About the author

Gordon F. Gibson was born in Vancouver in 1937. He attended the University of British Columbia (B.A., Honours, Mathematics and Physics '59) and Harvard Business School (MBA, Distinction '61), and subsequently did research work in political science at the London School of Economics.

He has been involved in a number of businesses, including prefabricated buildings, hotels, and real estate development, and has served on the boards of several public companies.

In politics, he served as Assistant to the Minister of Northern Affairs (1963-68), was Executive and later Special Assistant to the Prime Minister (1968-72), and ran in three federal elections. He was elected to the Legislature of B.C. in 1974, and served as both MLA and Leader of the B.C. Liberal Party (1975-79).

Since then, he has been active in both business and public affairs in western Canada, including 12 years on the Canada West Council. With Canada West, he co-authored *Regional Representation* (1981), authored *What if the Wheels fall off?: The case for a Constituent Assembly* (1992), and served on the Task Force on National Unity (1991-93).

Note to the Second Printing

THIS SECOND PRINTING HAS BEEN slightly modified to more precisely relate text and tables in two places, and clarify language in one other instance, as well as to add this note and an update of Michael Walker's preface.

Let me begin by thanking the readers of this book for the many comments received in respect of the first printing.

I write this the day after the September 12 election victory of the Parti Quebecois. The events covered in Chapter 2 have now begun. Throughout the country, there is a gradual awakening to a genuine crisis in our affairs. Over the next few months, the resourcefulness and determination of the separatists in Quebec will be better understood. International markets will understand sooner than most, and economic alarms will merge with the emotional stress of a nation under seige. Gradually, the popular press will acknowledge that the unthinkable could happen. They will predate official Ottawa by months in this regard, and lag reality by an even longer period.

A general requirement has been expressed for greater detail on "Plan C," which is the general solution proposed in Chapter 10. The presentation only of broad outlines in this book was not an oversight. When it was written, and even today, most Canadians simply cannot bring themselves to believe that anything remotely like "Plan C"—massive decentralization—is necessary. There was, and is, no point in asking people to focus on the details of fire prevention if they don't believe a

x

fire is possible. Ottawa has been very successful in convincing Canada (outside of Quebec) that there is no problem.

This book—*Plan B*—says that a problem exists, that it is of a magnitude to bring wrenching changes to our lives if not resolved, and that the resolution will restructure Canada beyond our current beliefs. All of that will be conventional wisdom within a few months, and it will be time enough then for "Plan C." The second reason for the lack of "Plan C" detail is based in well-founded humility. Writers can propose; history disposes. A new constitution, new rules (if we find them) for living together in this magnificent part of the world, must be broadly acceptable to most of us. And yet, we have hardly begun to talk. Our Charlottetown, our Meech—these were dialogues of the deaf elites. It is now well established that any new constitution must be "referendum proof." We must buy in massively, or it will not fly.

That kind of achievement sounds daunting, but it has been done many times in the past, by people under greater strain than we have known until now. "Plan C" must evolve from a process to which we all agree, if we ever get a chance to do so. Gaining that chance must be the focus for now—a collective cry to stop, and listen to Canada.

For reasons this book will elaborate, the odds of sorting things out in an intelligent way are very long indeed. It will require a determination that Canada is more important than Ottawa. Everyone outside of Ottawa will agree, but the gatekeepers to necessary reform will hold sway on Parliament Hill as long as they can, and that may be too late.

The alternative in this land is *not* just Parizeau or the status quo. There is a better way.

We will be giving our own details on "Plan C" in the months ahead. May those thoughts be a small part of a growing chorus. For now, the task is this: believe in Canada. The problem is not Quebec. The problem is Ottawa. That is our trap; that is our challenge. Chapter 2, which starts just after the September 12 election victory of the PQ is titled "The Beginning . . . of the End?" The question mark in that phrase is important: it could instead be the beginning of something better.

Gordon Gibson
Vancouver, September 13, 1994

Preface:
A First Draft of the
Future History of Canada

THIS IS AN IMPORTANT BOOK. It will evoke strong and varied responses. That is what is intended.

This is also a constructive book, one which tries to produce a positive outcome from what at the moment appears to be a dismal prospect. Many who share the author's concerns and his desire to arrive at a constructive alternative will disagree with the dour depiction of future events or the likely reactions to them. Some will think that Quebec electoral events will be different from those depicted in this book. Others will have a different view of the appropriate reaction by the rest of Canada in the event that Quebec does indeed decide to separate from the current federation.

Some of those who read this book have information that would lead them to take a different approach in constructing the economic and political scenarios that form the core of the book.

Every Canadian who reads the book will have a reaction of some kind.

For these reasons, we are regarding this as the first draft of the future history of the rest of Canada. The second draft, if necessary, will be published after the Quebec election of 1994 and will incorporate the suggestions and comments we receive on the first draft. If you, the

reader, would like to influence that next draft, please let us know how
you feel.

Why are we publishing this book?

Canadians are suffering from constitutional fatigue. They are also increasingly intolerant* towards the aspirations of Quebec separatists and
a historically high fraction of them want to have the issue settled "once
and for all." Such attitudes are apparently predicated on the notion that
Quebec's concerns are not legitimate and/or that the rest of Canada has
already "given enough" to Quebec. National leaders are taking a wait-
and-see posture based on the belief that the election in Quebec is not
about separation and that it is, in any event, a Quebec affair. In consequence, the only clear vision of the future of Canada is being articulated
by a political party designed to destroy it. The result is increasing
anxiety in financial markets and a large economic cost for the country.

We believe that this combination of attitudes is dangerous and is
predicated on insufficient consideration of the consequences for the rest
of Canada if the Parti Québécois wins the election. The most important
motivation for publishing this book is to stimulate public discussion
about the implications for the rest of Canada if that happens. The
urgency of this discussion is made clear by the fact that the leaders of
both the Parti Québécois and the Liberals have confirmed that they think
the election in Quebec is about separation.

There has been ample consideration of the economic impact on
Quebec and the rest of Canada if Quebec leaves. The Fraser Institute has
published three books on this topic: *Federalism in Peril* (1992), *The Economic Consequences of Quebec Sovereignty* (1991), and *Canadian Confederation at the Crossroads* (1978). All of these studies, as well as those done
by others, implicitly assume that the rest of Canada will carry on as a
country if Quebec leaves. In this book, Gordon Gibson explicitly con-
siders how likely this is to happen.

---

*   Angus Reid, Public Opinion Poll, published in the *Vancouver Sun*, June 3
     and June 4, 1994.

Pivotal to the future of the rest of Canada is the role that Ontario would play in the federation that remained. In such a federation, Ontario would have 51.8 percent of the GDP and nearly fifty percent of the population. As such, it would have the preponderance of the political influence and indeed, if the parliament were to be structured as it is now, nearly a clear majority in the House of Commons. Would the rest of the provinces happily reside in such a federation? What would be the economic and political consequences if they decided not to carry on with present arrangements? What new agreement might be necessary?

While the scenarios that emerge from such questions are indeed grotesque, they must be considered as we approach what could be the final debate about the future of the country. We must think the unthinkable if we are to approach the coming election in Quebec with the appropriate degree of gravity. We in the rest of Canada must abandon the attitude of this-is-an-issue-for-the-people-of-Quebec. It is an issue for every Canadian and we can influence how our fellow Canadians in Quebec feel by beginning now the public debate in the rest of Canada about what our attitudes, bargaining positions, and future prospects are likely to be if Quebec does indeed vote to elect a separatist government.

We should make no mistake about the fact that it is increasingly likely that if the Parti Québécois wins the upcoming election, it will immediately begin the process of preparing for separation. It has said as much in its published platform literature which it has taken the trouble to publish in English so that there can be no doubt in the rest of Canada about its intentions. We should take the separatists at their word. It will be too late to begin a discussion of the contents of this book at that time—we should do it now.

What does the book say?

While we would wish that every Canadian read this entire book, in reality many will not have the time or the inclination. In anticipation of that possibility, the author has summarized the essential conclusions of the "Plan B" deliberations in Chapter 9. His constructive alternative, "Plan C," is contained in Chapter 10. To get the full flavour of the discussion, the reading of Chapter 9 should be supplemented by dipping into the other chapters since the summary arguments could not have been arrived at without the scenarios developed in the text.

The central contention of this book is that while Quebec is the current focus of discussion, it is not the main problem the rest of Canada faces. The problem we face is that current constitutional arrangements are unstable and if Quebec leaves they will be unsustainable. Much as everybody dislikes the prospect, a win for the Parti Québécois is going necessitate the constitutional rethinking of the rest of Canada. We need to have a clear idea of our next best alternative to no deal with Quebec. That alternative is "Plan B."

The main points suggested by a consideration of "Plan B" are:

1. If the Parti Québécois is elected the federal government may well lose its legitimacy as a representative of the rest of Canada in any subsequent dealings. It has limited time in which to play a constructive role.

2. The main loser in a renewed rest of Canada will be what Gibson calls, "the Ottawa system," since keeping the rest of Canada together will require a much looser federation in which the central government will have very little power.

3. While there are some potential winners from the collapse of Canada, all of the "Plan B" configurations are inferior for a majority of Canadians and many of them are catastrophic for some regions.

4. Since saving the rest of Canada will require a major constitutional restructuring anyway, we should do it now with Quebec's involvement and save Canada. This is "Plan C" for Canada.

5. Because it will inevitably be a major loser under such a plan, it is unlikely that Ottawa is going to lead such a process of reform; Gibson proposes that a Constituent Assembly be struck to formulate a Constitution that will be acceptable to all parts of Canada.

What conclusions should be drawn?

The conclusion to be drawn from Gibson's careful construction of these alternative futures is that in a very real sense Ottawa, not Quebec, is the problem. Ottawa, which has so much to lose under any conceivable restructuring of Canada, has steadfastly refused to accord to all of the provinces the degree of decentralization of power that would satisfy Quebec, and which the rest of Canada will have to adopt if Quebec leaves. In this rigid adherence to the well-meaning, even if self-serving, notion that a strong central government is essential to our future, Ottawa imperils that future. It is time for federal politicians to recognize the extremely precarious position in which this inflexible centralist stance places the country.

Ottawa must act now to facilitate a Constituent Assembly so that its deliberations are substantially under way by the time the election in Quebec is held. This will convey to the people of Quebec a sense that a vote against separation in their province is not a vote against meaningful reform, which will come anyway from the Constituent Assembly in which it will play a role.

If Ottawa does not start the Constituent Assembly process, or some other process of meaningful reform that it does not control, then other parties such as the provincial premiers—including the premier of Quebec—should initiate the Assembly.

Perhaps a Constituent Assembly is not the answer, or perhaps the existing political structure is not the correct source from which it should spring. Perhaps there are other approaches to constructing a new vision for Canada. We hope that this book will stimulate their discovery because it is clear that the status quo is both dangerous and unlikely to persist, whatever happens in the Quebec election.

Michael A. Walker

Dedication

To my Kilby, and my country.

Chapter 1:
Introduction—The need
for a "Plan B"

W E CAN LEARN FROM OTHERS. In June of 1990, an opinion poll taken in the then-nation of Czechoslovakia[1] showed that only 5 percent of Czechs and 8 percent of Slovaks supported the idea of their country splitting up. Only two years later, in the fall of 1992, the proportion favouring separation reached almost 50 percent in both areas, and over 80 percent of both Czechs and Slovaks agreed that separation was inevitable. By the beginning of 1993, the deed was done. A strong separatist government in the smaller and poorer Slovakia,[2] and the wealthier Czech population next door each considered their own interests, and said goodbye.

Every situation is different, and the only lesson suggested here is that political events can develop with dazzling speed. Not to alarm, but in an abundance of caution, one must look ahead. This book, which

---

1   Robert A. Young, *The Breakup of Czechoslovakia*, sections II-ii and IV-iii. To be published by the Institute of Intergovernmental Relations, Queen's University, forthcoming.

2   The Czech Republic has a population of about 10 million. Slovakia is about half of that.

thinks about the previously unthinkable in Canada, was written for that first, main reason—to plan for a possible future.

If Quebec decides in a clear and democratic way to separate, it is essential that the rest of Canada have a blueprint of the options and procedures for formulating new arrangements not just with Quebec— which is the easier part—but also among ourselves in the much larger part of Canada outside of Quebec. There are no guarantees that there will be only *one* new country.

A second reason for thinking about Canada emerges during this examination. One arrives at the possibility that there may be a better solution for *everyone* (including Quebec separatists) than a full and final break. The favourite game of the separatist leaders is to tell their voters that they are trapped in a box, and the choice is simple. They can have the hated status quo, or independence. But that is not true. There are other options which might be better for us all.

The outline of this book assumes first a separatist victory in the 1994 Quebec elections, and a subsequent affirmative vote to secede. We then work through the main options for the probable rearrangement of our country under the new circumstances. This is "Plan B." It is not a happy thing for most of the country. If we don't like what we see, there is another way, a "Plan C." By happy chance, if "B" stands for "Break," then "C" stands for "Continuity"—but also for "Change."

"Plan A," of course, is what we have today. It is the natural job of the government of Canada to try to maintain the viability of that plan. But should that prove impossible, we will need another. That is the work of the pages that follow.

If you read this in 1994, you can approach it as political fiction or a version of future history, depending on your assessment of the probabilities. If you read it after the Quebec election and referendum have been held, the proper approach will be obvious.

Some very important people have told us it is foolish or wrong to talk about such things—or, certainly, at least not now. One hopes they are right, that there is no problem. But just on the small chance that they are wrong, or if they are right today but the issue comes back to haunt us every five or ten years, then we should be talking about it now.

Political earthquakes

There is a very human temptation not to worry about future problems, especially if they are seen as both improbable and drastic. Perhaps that is why there has been very little writing within ROC[3] in this area, especially on the touchy question as to whether the rest of Canada could survive as a unit. But we have had a wake-up call in the last federal election with the election of the Bloc Québécois as the clear representative in Ottawa of a majority of Quebeckers (and, by accident, the Official Opposition). The issue is now not merely timely, but urgent.

To draw an analogy with how the human mind works, recent earthquakes in California have led to a high degree of interest in earthquake planning in Canada, though of course we know not whether such an event will happen in the next year, or in the next millennium. The chances of a political earthquake in Quebec in the next year are much higher, and the consequences more severe. We should think about this.

For their own reasons, politicians outside of Quebec have almost universally declined this challenge. The reason is a good one for them: the subject is a no-winner, with no easy answers. And the very examination leaves a politician open to charges of disloyalty from opponents, on the grounds of giving credibility to an otherwise unthinkable event.

But that is not good enough. As a political community, there are two kinds of mistakes we can make here. The Type One mistake would be to go to the work and anguish of developing a plan for a very painful and complicated contingency that never happens. The cost to get started on that is a few tens of thousands of person-hours and a few millions of dollars, spread through the economy, plus perhaps some bruised feelings as we rigorously and dispassionately think through our options, priorities, and costs.

---

3   ROC is becoming the conventional abbreviation for the "rest of Canada." It is not pretty and with luck we will not need it for long, but it is better than CWQ—Canada without Quebec—or most other acronyms proposed to date. Albertans Bert and Alice Brown, founders of the very successful "Committee for a Triple-E Senate," suggest that "most of Canada" (MOC?) has a better ring. Newspaper editors will settle it for us.

The Type Two mistake would be to arrive at the point where we need a Plan B—but do not have one. That could be enormously expensive—well into the tens of billions with the assets and liabilities and international cash flows we are discussing. Things will be said and decisions will be made very quickly in the post-referendum period, if it is held and passes, that will have huge downstream implications and huge costs if the decisions are wrong. How do you calculate the cost of a Czechoslovakia? We must think about that in advance.

We receive new evidence every day from the countries of the former Soviet Union about what happens when you enter a new social and political order without a plan. Our problems would not be so large; we would not be required to go through an economic revolution at the same time as a political restructuring. But the problems would still be formidable.

Certainly the people of Quebec understand this. Whether most readers of this book think it is proper or not, there is a very extensive literature and body of thought within Quebec as to how that society will manage the process of separation, and its aftermath. Some of this is misleading or even dishonest, but there is a plan—indeed, there are many! These cover currency, trade patterns, government revenues and expenditures, legal frameworks, and other questions that will have to be answered, at least in principle and preferably in a lot of detail, before Quebeckers vote.

Quite apart from the downside of *not* having a plan, there are a couple of upsides to be gained from the exercise as well. The first is that "thinking about the unthinkable" may well play some part in preventing the unthinkable from happening. The classic example of this in the world politics of the past generation is Herman Kahn's *On Thermonuclear War*, published by the Hudson Institute. The work, which many people found extremely offensive even in principle, went through a very extensive modelling of who gets killed, where and when, as different scenarios of nuclear confrontation and various stages of war unfold in a hypothetical future.

The chilling thing was his ability coldly to contemplate levels of destruction and death that in some cases went into the billions, and talk about "winning" or "losing" such wars in a rational way. To many, this seemed just plain wrong, and so horrible that it had a good deal to do with the early momentum of the peace movement. And that is a second order illustration of the usefulness of the Kahn approach.

The first order of course is at the level of the decision-makers and strategists in the White House and Pentagon and in the Kremlin. They tried to think about all of these things, all of the time. The result (with the help of an unknown amount of luck) was that humanity got through that exceedingly dangerous Cold War era without anyone making an irrecoverable mistake. There were military Red Alerts, and we probably came closer than most of us will ever know. But no thermonuclear war was started by mistake, and the rational calculus of death developed by Kahn and others made it clear to those in charge of the launch button just how far they could push the other side, before the risks overshadowed the payoffs.

And if that was the first order effect, the second order was indeed the peace movement and other political ramifications of the nuclear "balance of terror," to use the phrase coined by Fred Soward of the University of British Columbia. In Cold War terms, the peace movement was a minus for our side because it constrained only the actions of the democracies, and had zero impact on the Soviets. The Cold War in the end was broken only by the internal weaknesses of the Soviet system, and the incredible pressures of the Reagan military build up on the politics and economics of Soviet society.

But some good came out of all of this. The world had been put through a generation of emotional experience that brought a more realistic approach to world problems. When Saddam Hussein invaded Kuwait, fast action was taken. There was little wringing of hands; it was clearly the thing to do. The number of nasty local conflicts around the world today indicates that we still have a lot to learn, but the experience of the Cold War did give a useful lesson in collective security.

In our own small Canadian way, a serious look at Plan B by enough of us should have both of these effects—helping to avoid mistakes today, and learning lessons for the future. Too many of us in ROC have dealt with a potential separation of Quebec in the same casual way that colonial powers dealt with war, before the think-tanks modelled the larger risks of modern military technology. The frequent comment in

ROC, of a separatist Quebec of, "Well then, let them go!" is neither a statement of benevolent laissez-faire, nor a carefully considered policy option. It is a knee-jerk reaction that does not weigh the consequences, as a Plan B must. In that sense, we need our strategists in the Kremlin and the Pentagon.

And on the second order effects, a serious look at the downside of Plan B could generate an opening of minds—a disposition in the country to reconsider some of the old ways and absolutist positions (such as "a strong central government," "official bilingualism from coast to coast," or "uniform national standards") that may no longer serve us so well.

In short, a serious consideration of Plan B may well lead us not in the direction of something worse, but of something *better*—call it "Plan C" for now. After all, for all of our appreciation for and pride in our country, it does have its problems. We do spend far too much time fighting each other on jurisdictional issues, instead of cooperating to solve problems. And we have spent so much money trying to paper over our internal regional and social tensions by economic bribery that our debt is, at worst, out of control, and at best, a truly crushing burden.

So far, our attempts to fix these relationship problems have failed. Indeed, it is apparent that the very things that make our political institutions a failure in many ways are also preventing us from fixing them. The gatekeepers to reform are those in charge of our governments, and they are mostly against change. It has been easier to claim that the old policies are really working—lots of kids in immersion schools and all that—and deny the defects, rather than invent new solutions.

And, of course, the gatekeepers to reform would be the losers by reform. In that sense, our real Canadian problem may lie far more in Ottawa than in Quebec City. This is a heretical thought for many, but if analysis shows that to be the case, there are many easier and less traumatic ways of fixing our country than by parting with Quebec.

We will find out about this if, and only if, the voters of Quebec require us to do so. It is certainly not the mood of the country voluntarily to spend much time on constitutional topics. The popular statement is that the problem of today is jobs. Of course, that is a problem throughout the industrialized world; the very ubiquity of the problem suggests that there are no easy solutions.

But the constitutional issue also has a whole lot to do with jobs, in less obvious ways. You can't run a proper economy or get the deficit under control when your main unspoken concern is keeping the country intact from one day to the next by whatever concessions are necessary, but this is exactly the dilemma of Ottawa today. That problem is not going to go away. It has been with us for a long time, and it will stay with us until it is resolved.

No government in Ottawa is going to touch this one voluntarily. It is a curious but true thing: it is very much up to the voters of Quebec as to whether this and all of the other divisive issues in the constitutional file are going to be left on the back burner or brought to centre stage.

Against the contingency that the voters of Quebec do just that, what follows is an approach to thinking through what the rest of us will then do. There is no reason to think that this exercise will be completely negative. To repeat: there is always the possibility that there may be a better solution for everyone, including Quebec separatists, than that of a full and final break. We will get to that after examining the difficulties that a break would bring for everyone.

Chapter 2:
The Beginning—of
the End?

THE INTRODUCTION SPOKE OF EARTHQUAKES. Human earthquakes are different from the physical variety. In nature, there is a sudden, sharp, damaging event, followed by a period of declining aftershocks. The earthquake hits hard, without warnings that we can detect, and then quickly dies away.

In human affairs, there is a series of pre-shocks, foreshadowing what is to come. Then we have the rupture, breaking past from future. This is the earthquake, which can be of obvious importance, or may seem almost a non-event at the time. Then come a series of increasingly violent consequences, which reach a crest and eventually subside to anequilibrium.

Most political earthquakes can be seen in this light, from the Russian revolution in 1917, through the encounter of Chamberlain and Hitler at Munich,[4] to the events that triggered the dissolution of Yugoslavia. Unlike natural earthquakes, the human kind can usually be foreseen, and either avoided or softened. But there finally comes a moment when

---

4   From which came the famous forecast of "Peace in our time!" In a very different context, the Ottawa assurance is, "No problem!"

the die is cast. Reversing the trend becomes extremely difficult and the costs rise exponentially.

The election of a second separatist government in Quebec would be just such a rupture. A subsequent affirmative referendum would almost certainly finish Canada as we know it.[5] The purpose of this chapter is to model those early days from the election to the referendum.

As of this writing the election is imminent, to be called in days, or at most, weeks. The polls are Delphic, to be read as you wish. The concentrations of strength, leading to "wasted votes" for one party or the other (but especially for federalists in anglophone areas), is a wild card. Each side claims it can win.

In any event, we assume a victory for the Parti Québécois. A surprise Liberal victory would leave everyone a great deal more time to reflect. It would defer many of the hard questions for a number of years, though they almost certainly would be back. But our task is to investigate the PQ victory hypothesis.

It is almost impossible today to exaggerate the feeling of concern in the country the day after a PQ victory. It would be quite the opposite of that other great protest vote, the Charlottetown Accord. The day after that, most people felt pretty good. We had won, after all. We had beaten the whole political establishment. It was a triumph of democracy, with the additional advantage of preserving the status quo rather than forcing Canadians to face a very uncertain future.

And the day after that vote, nothing changed. Life went on. The sky did not fall, as Brian Mulroney had told us. The dollar didn't fall, either. The big fall was reserved for Mr. Mulroney's party, but we didn't know that yet.

---

5   Nova Scotia voted to separate from the new Canada in 1867, just after the deal was done. The rest of the country simply ignored them and life went on. That was then and this is now. Still, this strategy has been seriously proposed. The difficulties are explored in Appendix 1.

A new situation

It will be quite different after a PQ victory. We will clearly be launched into a future largely uncharted. To use the imagery of the sea, we will all know in our bones that in spite of a lot of rocks and storms out there, we will have left on a perilous voyage, and we may or may not return to the old harbour. But at sea we shall be.

In Quebec there will be a mixture of jubilation and trepidation, with the former capturing the attention. The heady first days of a democratic adventure—for such it would certainly be—will give rise to an initial euphoria that could in fact be quite dangerous, in the sense of creating unrealistic expectations. Premier Parizeau and his crew will have a job to do, dampening these expectations on the one hand, while fanning the euphoria, in preparation for a referendum.

The new government will control the timing of a referendum in law, but not wholly in fact. They will have to conjure with the effects inside Quebec of the external world's reaction to their election. For example, should the financial markets of the world send unmistakably adverse signals through, say, a major slump in the value of Quebec Hydro bonds, that would be a negative. Should major political voices in ROC make irrationally bellicose statements of damn-the-torpedoes type economic warfare, that would be a negative. At some level of intensity, the new government would have to back off and take the time to attempt to repair the climate.

And of course ROC will have its problems too. In Ottawa there will be consternation, the government trying to find the right calming message without downplaying the important battle looming on the horizon, trying to rally Canadians without spooking foreign bankers. Embassies around Ottawa will be abuzz with cables demanding reports on the meaning of these developments. The U.S. Ambassador (and no one will really care what people in any other country think, except for Japanese bondholders) will solemnly affirm that this is a matter internal to Canada, and there is nothing else he or she can say. But some time previously the Americans will have dusted off *their* contingency studies on the breakup of Canada, which are no doubt far better than ours. This is a significant matter to our neighbours to the south, and they are cold-blooded about such things.

In provincial capitals, governments will actively begin to consult their own interests. The future will have suddenly become very unclear, and each provincial government will have a duty to plan for its citizens, at a minimum, and even to see if this situation could be turned to advantage. The nature of politics is coping with change, however unexpected and bizarre that change might be. The potential end of Canada as we know it is almost off the usual change charts, but politicians will have to cope nevertheless.

In financial centres around the world, investors will watch carefully and issue newsletters giving their measured assessments. (They will very often get the politics wrong, but the trillion dollars in currency trading that washes around the world every day does not care about these subtleties.) Their attention will constrain the more extreme rhetoric that might otherwise erupt in Quebec or Ottawa, for our financial situation could erode very quickly. We will have to remind ourselves frequently—as we should even today, whatever Quebec does—that the first consequence of being deeply in debt is a marked loss of autonomy.

Anyone who has ever seriously been in politics knows that success in that field comes as to a surfer, riding that uncontrollable wave for just a bit longer, and until you die, if you're lucky. The successful surfer senses a change in the sea, and we are talking a real sea change here. If it turns out that the new Quebec government can sell its referendum to its voters—if the mould is shattered—what will Albertans, for example, think? Premiers will not overlook that simple question.

In particular, studies will be fired up on the future of ROC. No government can afford to do such studies today, for it would soon become known and would generate enormous criticism. No government will be able to afford *not* to do such studies after a PQ government is elected. And the results of these studies, in economic terms at least, will range from depressing through to very hopeful. The progression on this scale will escalate with the degrees of longitude, east to west.

The problem of Ottawa

The tough place to be will be Ottawa. Since it has been such a cushy place to be for so long, no one will feel much sympathy about that, but it will be tough for the people who live there, be they politicians, public servants, or even federal pensioners, or those in the private sector.

Consider this: the first job—the *very* first job—of any organism, or any organization, is to preserve its existence. The day after a successful PQ election in Quebec, the Government of Canada will be seriously and actively challenged in that first duty. If you thought that Quebec was a priority in Ottawa before, just wait for this day!

The focus of the government of Canada will clearly be on Quebec. It will not be on ROC. We shall have to plan for ourselves. I underline this statement, and will return to it. Ottawa[6] is even today absorbed with the Quebec issue. After a PQ victory, they will be totally captured. They will have no time for contingency planning for ROC, and they will resent anyone raising the issue.

This is neither surprising, nor bad. The job of Ottawa at that point will be to try to defeat the referendum question of the PQ, for a "Yes" will essentially mean the end of Ottawa as we and they know it. Some of the motives will be as lofty as the languages of Shakespeare or Molière could describe. Others will be as base as the impending crash in Ottawa residential real estate if this deal passes. Never mind—one must take motives as they are. But one must also remember that the motives of Ottawa are mixed, and with the strong overlay of self-interest involved, the capital has a major conflict of interest in attempting to deal dispassionately with the future of Canada. Solutions which might be right for the rest of us but would hurt *Ottawa* might not get the attention they deserve.

To this end of defeating the referendum, all federal resources will be mobilized. The Charlottetown Accord propaganda will be nothing in comparison, but the whole effort will be in Quebec. The result will be a most illuminating snapshot of the politics of Canada: rough as we have

---

6   Here and elsewhere in the book, the reference to "Ottawa" should be taken to include much more than the government of the day. It is the whole system of power and control and networks that has not only run this country, but believes it is uniquely qualified to do so. The lives of thousands of well-informed and powerful people are in the balance here. This is not just a fight for Canada-as-we-know-it. This is deeply personal.

ever seen them, and then enlarged times ten. A Quebec vote in favour of independence will be one thing, to be analyzed further in this essay, for that is our task. If Ottawa manages to engineer a vote against independence, the mechanics will be an eye-opener for all of us, and that would be a fascinating book to write, full of dollars and duplicity, on all sides of the fence![7]

The referendum battle

The battle for the referendum will begin the day after a PQ election win. For its part, the government of Quebec will be going over well-tilled ground. They have done this before, after all, and have theories as to how to avoid losing again.

In the recently published English version of the party plan,[8] the program is clearly set out. The stages are:

- The National Assembly will pass a "solemn declaration stating Quebec's wish to accede to full sovereignty"
- Commence talks with the federal government to establish "the timetables and modalities for transferring powers and determine the rules for dividing Canada's assets and debts"
- Institute a Constitutional Commission to draw up a proposed constitution for a sovereign Quebec
- "As quickly as possible," call a referendum to pronounce on the sovereignty and new constitution. "This referendum will be the act that will bring into being a sovereign Quebec"
- Propose "mutually advantageous forms of economic association"

The Parti Québécois has made it quite clear that they are running on a platform of separation. They will take the election vote, if it goes in their favour, as a mandate in that direction. If the provincial Liberals

---

7   It is true that as at this writing, the polls say that any vote for independence is at least ten points short of a majority, so Ottawa's task looks easy. It is well to recall the opening words of this book, recording that a separatist movement in Slovakia was able to get its way in only two years, starting from a far lower base of support for separation than exists in Quebec today.

8   *Quebec in a New World*, Toronto: James Lorimer & Co., 1994.

also choose to fight the election as a quasi-referendum on the future of Quebec, then that view will be strengthened. That is why, at least so far, the federal authorities are characterizing the election almost as a non-event. They know it is not, but they want to be able to say that a PQ win is not a loss for them.

To the extent that the new PQ government will be able to claim a mandate for separation simply from the election, they will use this position to take every step in that direction short of an actual breach of existing Canadian law. This gives room for some very provocative acts, and, of course, any negative reaction by Ottawa or ROC (always remember—the two are not the same!) will be depicted as evidence of an attitude of arrogant rejection of the democratically-expressed will of Quebeckers.

Ottawa will deny this, but difficulties do exist. As the PQ is quite aware, the federal government may well decline to enter into pre-referendum talks of the kind promised in the PQ election manifesto. They may take the position that until a referendum has passed—which they will argue will never happen—there is nothing to discuss. The PQ will be able to use that refusal as further evidence of an anti-Quebec government in Ottawa ignoring the democratically expressed wishes of the voters at the recent election.

The statement in the PQ manifesto that a successful referendum per se would end Canada and institute a new country is full of legal holes and pitfalls, as the PQ well knows. Still, these things are governed more by politics than by law, and part of the game is to convince Quebeckers that this is all quite straightforward, no problem.

Thus, the "clear and coherent plan" contains comforting sections on the new Quebec constitution, Quebec citizenship, Territory, Continuity of Law, Continuity of Services to Individuals and Corporations, Division of Public Property and the Debt, International Relations, and Economic Association with Canada.

The plan is all very soothing, very logical, and very misleading. It is also selling to a great many Quebeckers as this book is being written. The challenge to the Parti Québecois government will be to keep and raise the comfort level in the runup to the referendum. Their essential messages to Quebeckers will be as follows:

The Quebec Argument

"Your standard of living will be safe."

For most voters, this will be *the* make-or-break issue. The PQ will have to offer believable assurances on jobs, pensions, UI, medicare, and various social programs. These discussions will extend to trade, currency, and the federal and provincial debt.

Much of the debate will take place in this area. Many of the assumptions employed by the separatists, and related studies such as that of the Bélanger-Campeau Commission, are based on such untenable positions as escaping with only 17 or 18 percent of the federal debt.[9]

This economic battlefield will also include strong arguments that Ottawa has proven its fiscal irresponsibility beyond any doubt, and that Quebec cannot afford to remain in such a system. Most of the arguments are well known—dairy subsidies, net value of transfer payments, et cetera—but this one of fiscal irresponsibility in Ottawa is worth some elaboration, since it is both relatively unknown outside of Quebec and outrageously unacceptable to ROC.

The PQ point is this: Quebec's own debt is bad enough, but it is coming under control, and in any event, was mostly incurred for useful purposes. On the other hand, they argue, *Ottawa's* debt has largely been incurred through a lack of self-discipline and fiscal mismanagement. Canada is entirely unable to acquire the necessary discipline and management until it is forced to so so by international financiers. Quebec must therefore cut itself loose from this financial disaster-in-waiting.

The average ROC voter, who is inclined to believe that the federal debt has come about mostly as a result of bribes to Quebec—though this is a serious over-statement, the Atlantic being a larger factor in this regard—becomes apoplectic at this point. But nevertheless, the argument sells in Quebec.

The PQ will argue that the interests of ROC require, and guarantee, sensible cooperation to ensure a smooth transition. This is the "heads-

---

9   For an excellent analysis of these issues, see Patrick Grady, *The Economic Consequences of Quebec Sovereignty*, Vancouver: The Fraser Institute, 1991.

I-win-tails-you-lose" approach to ROC threats. Quebeckers will be told that these folks in ROC are really rational people, and no matter what they say in the heat of today, they will follow their own interests—to work with us in a new relationship.

"Your new country will be secure."

This will include discussions of borders (no change, of course), international alliances, and proposed defence agreements with the United States. The basic argument will be that continuity will prevail in everything, except that Quebec City will now do all the things formerly done by Ottawa. This alleged continuity will be grounded in arguments about international law, and the self-interest of others (especially the United States, but including ROC), in getting along with the new order. There are counter-arguments of course, but the game of the parties here is not to seek the truth: it is to win.

It will be difficult for voices outside Quebec to counter these arguments. To predict uncertainty, chaos, possible violence, self-determination for Quebec minorities, and extremely difficult bargaining sessions on all matters will be seen in Quebec as fear-mongering, an unworthy tactic in itself which simply invites an emotional and defiant response.[10] However, silence will be interpreted as conceding the power and merit of the continuity arguments. Either way, the pro-referendum forces have an edge.

We will return to this in chapter 5, particularly to the matter of borders, the most explosive of issues.

"Our language and culture will finally be safe, once we have all the tools of a national state."

This is the core of the separatist position, and it will be invoked with such fervent passion and emotional enthusiasm as to seem almost

---

10   Of course, if you can provoke *enough* fear, you win, at least for now. This will be an interesting test of our layers of civility.

bizarre outside the province. Quebec will present itself as the threatened victim of a grimly assimilationist anglophone continent, and federalism will be the set of hobbles that prevents a meaningful response. The federal government and the Supreme Court will be the subversive influences that undercut the well-intentioned and necessary measures of cultural self-protection.

At the same time, the separatist forces will almost certainly offer strong reassurances to anglophones and allophones, blaming such transient incidents as the sign law on the baleful influence of a limiting federalism, rather than being an indication of the natural tolerance of the Quebec community. And since the possibility of a mass out-migration is one of the greatest threats to the prosperity of an independent Quebec, there will be major reassurances. Thus, curiously, we shall probably see stronger guarantees for the English language within Quebec than we have today. The juxtaposition of these two elements will seem so paradoxical to many Canadians that it will be hard even to frame a reply, but the package is extremely important to the sovereignt-ist argument.

"An independent Quebec will be set free from the built-in inefficiencies of Canada. This, taken together with the enthusiasm and energies released at the outset of a new nation-state, will underwrite a growing prosperity."

Here much will be made of the natural resources of the province, its world class business capabilities, and so on. It is an item of faith for Quebeckers, something they have heard so often as to put beyond question, that their provincial economy is an important engine of Canadian economic growth—so much so that it can easily stand alone. Yes, there is high unemployment, but this tends to be the fault of the feds.

These will be the major components of the positive side of the "sell" within Quebec, buttressed by reports, analyses and comparative studies showing glowing prospects after independence. We can expect to hear a great deal about the world's most prosperous and successful economies in the 6 to 10 million population range, and a similar amount about the cultural and economic vigour of "la francophonie."

The negative side of the sell, which will start in a more muted fashion but will build through the campaign, especially if the polls do not look good for separatism, will pick up on every negative episode from the past century. We will hear about the conscription crisis, Quebec's isolation and indeed betrayal in the 1982 constitution decisions, and Quebec's humiliation in and after Meech Lake. The famous television clip of Brockville goons stomping on the Quebec flag is without doubt still carefully preserved on videotape, and will be joined by any new incidents of that kind.

Emotional appeals and historic grievances loom as large on any nationalistic agenda as economic issues. For this reason, both the Bloc Quebecois and the PQ will work very hard to provoke, and then exploit, angry and hostile outbursts from English Canada, of which some elements do not require a lot of provocation.

Ottawa's dilemma

The federalist forces will presumably take the opposite side of each of these propositions. Much of the strategy is straightforward, and there is much to work with. That does not mean that the task is easy, however, for these issues are terribly complicated, and in many cases one who is being honest must say they just don't know how this or that ball will bounce. In such a situation, the winner tends to be the side that most people consider trustworthy. Ottawa has a problem here, and not just in Quebec.

Much more difficult than the factual dialogue for Ottawa will be the following questions.

To what extent should the battle be left to the Quebec federalists, and to what extent should Ottawa take part directly?

At the time of the 1980 referendum, the political climate was somewhat different. The PQ had been in government for quite a while, and the provincial Liberal opposition, which led the federalist side of the debate, was in vigorously good shape. This time around, under our assumption, a tired Liberal provincial government with a new unproven leader will just have lost. This is a weakness.

At the time of the last referendum, the overwhelming majority of Quebec MPs in Ottawa were federalists, mostly Liberals. This time, there are only a few Liberals, mostly from anglophone ridings, and the overwhelming majority of Quebec MPs are separatists. This too is a weakness, and a big one.

So should the government in Ottawa unabashedly take the lead? Or would this backfire? It is a risk, though the government would probably conclude that it would have no choice but to pull out all the stops. But when the basic issue is trust, Ottawa does not start with a commanding lead, in Quebec or anywhere else in the country.[11]

To what extent will the dialogue go beyond rational argument to the use of scare tactics and/or threats?

If Ottawa can believably say, "If you separate, ROC will not only not be your friend, it will be your enemy," then this is a powerful argument whether one likes it or not. But the question of believability could be difficult, at least in the longer term, as such an attitude would be irrational, and somewhat costly to ROC. It is one thing to say that $1.35 billion in effective annual subsidies to Quebec dairy farmers will disappear.[12] It is quite another to say that the huge and profitable trade in goods and services across the Quebec-Ontario border would end. And there are many commercial entities that have substantial economic interests on each side of that line.

---

11   Although Prime Minister Chrétien is much liked, especially outside of Quebec, in assessing such fundamental questions as these on the constitution, people will tend to consider past behaviour. It is part of the folklore of much of Quebec that Ottawa has systematically betrayed the province over time, and a referendum period is too short to change this.

12   "Agricultural Policies, Markets and Trade," *Monitoring Outlook 1992*, Paris: OECD, 1992.

Then there is the more specific matter of the exact borders of Quebec. Claims can be made on behalf of ROC for particular parts of Quebec, especially the James Bay-Ungava region, including most of the giant James Bay hydro project, but also including the south shore of the St. Lawrence. For ROC, these claims would carry the additional emotional force of the interests of (mostly anglophone) natives in the north and a land corridor to the Maritimes in the south.

This again is a powerful card, but one fraught with danger. Again, the key is believability. The government of Quebec, through its agents (including the provincial police), has effective occupation of this territory. Since the matter of boundaries is a totally non-negotiable issue for the PQ, and indeed for most Quebeckers,[13] any Ottawa threat to remove territory would have to include a credible threat to use the military against Quebeckers, possibly in support of native insurrections. Such a threat would dramatically change conditions, alienating some voters who would have otherwise opposed the referendum, and capturing others through fear. It would also place some very unwelcome strains on military personnel, who were not recruited to fire bullets at Canadians.

The federal government could suggest other unfriendly steps it might take. That independence would end subsidies and transfer payments to Quebec goes without saying, but the balance here is not large. Indeed, the balance of federal cash into Quebec is "only" about $3 billion[14] after netting taxes into Ottawa and payments back to Quebec. (This excludes interest payments on the public debt held by residents of or institutions in the province of Quebec, as one should, and of which the lion's share of payments are made to Ontario in any case.)

Beyond this, however, is the whole issue of trade. ROC could, though not easily, stand the pain of cancelling commerce with Quebec,

---

13   When federal Indian Affairs Minister Ron Irwin suggested in May of 1994 that natives in northern Quebec would be able to take their lands and stay in Canada if they wished, Liberal Premier Johnson found it necessary to *immediately* state that, no matter what, Quebec's boundaries are unalterable.

14   *Government Spending Facts 2*, The Fraser Institute, 1994.

and it would hurt the latter more. However, this would also beggar many ROC business investments in Quebec. And if Quebec were admitted to GATT on its own application, or argued for successor status in GATT equally with ROC or its parts, it might win, in which case discrimination would be a violation of GATT.

The NAFTA issue is another area where Ottawa might be able to make trouble for Quebec, at least as a threat during the pre-referendum period. Whether any of these fights would make sense post-referendum is quite another question—a fact which will, of course, be exploited by the PQ.

If the Liberal government is on the line in these matters, what about the Reform Party? Will it sign on to the Liberal battle plan, either because it will subordinate its own interest to larger matters, or because it fears any other action will be seen as treasonous? Will it continue to market its own version of a "new Canada"? Will it talk past the referendum, and prepare itself as a rallying point for ROC opinion if and when the referendum succeeds? These are tough choices. There is room for more than one hot seat in Ottawa, but if Reform captures the spirit of ROC better than the Liberals on this most important of issues, then the Liberals could go the way of the Conservatives. This is a deadly game.

ROC versus Ottawa

So where does all of this leave us? The work of the Government of Quebec is to make a reasonable case for independence, buttressed by emotion and national pride. The work of Ottawa is to undermine this case, by a combination of rational argument and fear-mongering.

And where does all of this leave ROC? ROC and Ottawa are not the same things at all. One cannot emphasize this too strongly. "Ottawa" is a set of specific interests that are paid for by all Canadians, but really work for themselves. The first rule is personal and institutional survival, the second is politics, and a mere third is the common good. This is not a criticism; it is a statement of fact about governments everywhere. The trick is to make *their* interests roughly coincide with *ours*.

This point is worth a mid-chapter reality check. When you think about it, what is the Government of Canada? It is the collective voice of Canadians on certain issues, as spelled out in the constitution. However—and this is very clear in our law and history—it is only *one* voice on the constitution itself, which in law and practice until 1992 was a creature of the provincial level of government as well. It remains that, with the important addition of a voice for the people. It is now unthinkable that fundamental changes would be made without popular approval as indicated in a referendum.

Moreover, under the circumstances assumed here, it is clear that the current federal government cannot speak for *Canada* on constitutional issues, even at the federal level, save in a narrow legal sense. Why not? First, it was elected on a mandate that explicitly had nothing to do with constitutional matters. It has refused to talk about the constitution. Its mandate, stated over and over, has to do with "jobs"—and certainly not the constitution.

More importantly, and to the extent that it might be argued that the implicit mandate of any federal government has to do with national unity (and I agree with this), how does it deal with this case? How does it deal with a question where the Parliament of Canada is fractured along provincial lines and along Government/Official Opposition lines on the question of separation?

The Government of Canada clearly cannot claim to speak for a majority of Quebeckers, even now, and it certainly will not be able to do so after a successful PQ election victory. It can plausibly claim to be the voice of the Atlantic provinces on these matters, and of Ontario as well, though not to the extent that 97 out of 99 MPs would indicate. And the Government of Canada cannot particularly claim to speak for Alberta and British Columbia, where Reform obtained far more seats and far more votes.

Now, if *Parliament* can be made to speak with one voice (save the Bloc), then this is a much more powerful grouping—but it is still not ROC. More fundamentally, what is in question here is Canada in all its parts, not just Parliament. In such a case, the constituent parts become plenary speakers in their own right. The provincial governments are the logical vehicles at first blush, but they were not elected with this matter in mind, any more than were the MPs in Ottawa, except for the Bloc Quebecois. So, as was the case in the debate on the Charlottetown Accord, legitimate voices will proliferate far beyond the usual suspects.

And where will the ordinary citizens of ROC outside of Ottawa (ROCOOO?)—who are the true owners of this deal, after all—be in all of this? Surely not silent, as much as politicians might prefer it that way. Every open line show and editorialist from coast to coast will have views, and frequently. The classic stages of grief will be in full view, though how many will get all the way from denial, through anger and bargaining, to acceptance within an allowed time frame is another question.

The rest of the world

The loudest voices, the easiest to understand, and the ones that the Quebec leadership may find useful to dignify by emotional response, will be the voices of anger. The voices of calm consideration will take longer to be heard, and will always suffer in the decibel rating. There will also be a constant sub-theme of more narrowly focused voices, of how-can-we-turn-this-to-advantage, that will criss-cross the battlefield depending upon their shifting assessments of the future. The government of Quebec may take this into account in considering its timing, for surely the *vox populi* of ROC will be important to them.

But there is another timing factor, alluded to earlier. As all of this unfolds, the rest of the world will be watching. Most will look on with benign indifference, for in the great sweep of history, this is not the stuff to stir the soul of your average German or Bangladeshi. The truly interested parties, apart from the diplomats, will be the aforesaid foreign owners of our government bonds and notes, and their daily appraisal will be of great importance to us all.

None of these people care whether Canada stays together. What they care about is whether they will get paid their interest on time, and their principal when it is due. Whether payment comes from the Canada of today, a consortium of provinces, or a successful takeover group headed by the Sultan of Brunei, it matters not a whit to them. But *risk* and *uncertainty* do matter. At a small risk, they merely charge more. At a high risk, they bail out. And as Ottawa, Quebec City, and every other serious player knows, the perception of risk depends directly on whether those involved will respect the debt obligations unconditionally.

This is a powerful constraint. Recall once again to what extent we are dependent on our daily transfusion of fiscal blood from abroad, however tainted, to feed our standard-of-living habit. If the required $70 million per day (365 days per year)[15] dries up, we will need to replace it at far higher interest rates—or chop our standard of living. It really is that simple. One might think that this would inject a note of caution, but as Humpty Dumpty said to Alice,[16] "when I use a word, it means just what I choose it to mean." In that spirit, the separatists would explain such a problem as a failure of management by Ottawa, providing yet one more reason for a quick exit.

On the other side, what could be a greater argument for federalism than a collapse in the dollar and a surge in interest rates as a result of the Quebec crisis? Yes—but dangerous waters for fishing. These things can easily go too far, nudging parts of ROC and/or Quebec voters to say, "Let's get out of this!"

And this is not all. The ordinary life of our economy sees a constant ebb and flow of investment, always accommodating to new technology, new ideas, and the opportunities of the day. With sufficient uncertainty, this kind of thing stops. It costs nothing on day one or day two, but in due course the cumulative effects hurt—a lot.

In the interregnum between a successful PQ election and the holding of the referendum, life must go on. Ordinary issues must be addressed if they are urgent, Parliaments and Legislatures must be summoned, Question Period met, and budgets passed. And every single event will become one more issue in the Quebec Question. Things will edge towards paralysis and uncertainty will grow. Is there an obvious way out?

No—not unless the public opinion polls indicate a clear trend towards rejection of the independence option by Quebec voters. Under our hypothesis, two powerful governments will have their total resources dedicated to wooing the voters of one province. Each will work

---

15   This is the approximate daily inflow of foreign funds required to balance out our Current Account deficit with the rest of the world.

16   *Through the Looking Glass*, of fond memory.

to destabilize the other, within the constraints of the willingness of the public and the outside financiers to tolerate such things.

Solutions that won't be used

There are, however, a couple of *highly unconventional* ways out that Ottawa might consider if it gets hot enough. Remember that Canadians hate uncertainty and disorder. This is a very human characteristic but, along with a few other of the more staid peoples of the earth, we have raised it to an art form. While we say we are a market society, for us even the benign (in the aggregate) chaos of the marketplace must be thoroughly tamed and tempered. This is one of the ways we differ from New York or Hong Kong, being closer to Stockholm or Tokyo in this sense. So we might put a lot of pressure on Ottawa to "do something!"

It would take a lot of pressure, because the two best "somethings" that Ottawa could do would both require a clear acceptance that the old order is dead, including the pre-eminence of the federal government, and that is tough. But either route would vastly increase the chances of saving Canada.

The first and best would be to convene a Constituent Assembly from all across the country, which would, in effect, attempt to design a Canada in which Quebec would be happy. Constituent Assemblies have a long and successful history in the constitution-making of this planet. The machinery is outlined in some detail in a later Chapter, as it can be used at a later point in the unfolding crisis. The sad fact is that it is most unlikely to be used between the Quebec election and the referendum when it would most certainly stop the clock on separation and open the way to a renewed Canada.

The federal government would not like the idea because it would lose control of the agenda, and the constitution of the country. The Parti Québécois would not like the idea because it would be a terrible threat to separatism that they could not ignore. Neither side would like those consequences.

The public of English Canada might not like the timing either, because it could be represented as giving into Quebec yet one more time—just by accepting the concept of changing Canada enough that a separatist-minded province would remain.[17] In this attitude we would be foolish, but human nature being what it is, it may take a good deal of misery before people decide that something is better than nothing, when the continued existence of Canada is in play. So, the likelihood is that both sides would rather roll the dice on a winner-take-all, than adopt a solution where everybody gets some.

Unlike a Constituent Assembly, which can still be used down the road to good effect (see Chapter 8), the other unconventional solution is really much better used at this point. It is the solution of a law on *partition*.

Law on separation

In one of the most imaginative and remarkable books produced on this subject,[18] Scott Reid, an Ottawa journalist, has proposed a solution that would have a good chance of working at a time like this. Its advantages are that it would make separation somewhat less likely, and very much more civilized if it did proceed. Its disadvantage is that it would legitimize the concept of separatism, and require the federal government and ROC (for the provinces would have to agree as well), and indeed public opinion as well, to explicitly accept that.

In developing his idea, Reid reviews in detail secessionist experiences in Ireland, Yugoslavia, and Switzerland. The latter is the only one that worked, in examples as early as 1597 and as recently as 1979 (the Jura—Berne split). In the most recent case, the institution of a law on partition defused a situation that had become extremely tense and somewhat violent as well.

The core of the concept is this: we accept that separatist tendencies exist, and therefore we put in place a law to regulate such an event. The essence of the law is that a legitimate separation can only occur through

---

17 An Angus Reid survey taken in June 1994 showed that 46 percent of the ROC residents polled considered themselves becoming "more hardline" over the past year, compared to only 6 percent who thought themselves "more sympathetic."

18 *Canada Remapped*, Vancouver: Arsenal Pulp Press, 1992.

an expression of the will of the people on the basis of rather small units. In Reid's model, he proceeds on a poll-by-poll basis,[19] and on an analysis of linguistic data concludes that a democratic vote would result in about 700,000 citizens, mostly in West Montreal, deciding to carve themselves out of the existing Quebec, and connect themselves to Ontario by a corridor.

Other than that, there would be relatively few "enclave" problems, and the probable results make some geographic sense. The largest imponderable is northern Quebec, and here the districting and the views of natives become very important. (For voting purposes it is interesting to note that of the territory ceded to Quebec by Canada in the laws of 1898 and 1912, some 80 percent of the population is now francophone.)

Reid deals quite successfully with how would-be separatists are trapped by their own democratic logic, and that works—*if* the law is in place prior to Quebec's own, province-wide referendum. It becomes much more difficult after that. The idea is worth a very careful look, especially by the federal authorities. Do not hold your breath on this one, however.

Violence

There is one other thing that might derail a referendum campaign—or give it a boost. It is a wild card, in every sense of the word. The issue is serious violence during the referendum period.

Canadians hate violence. Quebeckers share that view. The reaction of the authorities to violence has tended to overwhelming counter-force—even excessive some would say. The famous examples are the Winnipeg General Strike of 1919, the unemployed trekkers in Regina in 1935, and the War Measures Act in Quebec in 1970. Each deployed massive force; each gained overwhelming public support. (The Oka

---

19   Reid goes on the basis of simple majority, poll by poll. An alternative approach is that of a *supermajority*, either overall (say 60 percent), or a simple majority of votes in a *supermajority of polls or ridings*—say between 60 and 70 percent. This helps defuse the enclave issue.

confrontation with the military in 1990 may show a change in this trend. Military force was deployed, but there was absolutely no disposition to actually *use* it, in the sense of breaking heads or shooting bullets. Whether this was driven by political correctness or a new attitude towards use of official force is not yet clear.)[20]

If serious violence should arise during the pre-referendum period (blockades leading to deaths, kidnappings of notables, downing of aircraft, explosion of major buildings)—the results would be absolutely unforeseeable. If massive force were needed, would a PQ government ever ask the feds for help? If Ottawa moved into an area where it felt no need of an invitation—say to assist a native community in the north or a federal military installation in Quebec City—what would this do to the politics of the referendum? Would it frighten order-loving Quebeckers into playing it safe and voting "No"? Or would it simply goad them into voting "Yes" to show support for their own authorities in dealing with internal violence in their own way?

Isolated hotheads may be planning this sort of provocative incident right now. We will hope the authorities have contingency plans, and equally hope they will never be needed. And if we do have to face violence, there will be a role for the public as well, to which we return in the chapter on "Attitude," which makes or breaks this whole unfolding drama and moves it up or down the continuum from bearable, through unfortunate, to tragic.

If none of the above surprises happen, then the stresses of uncertainty will escalate as we approach the day of a Quebec referendum, though heavily conditioned by what the pollsters are telling us on any given day. If and when a new Parti Québécois government starts the referendum train down the tracks, we may be sure it will have chosen the most propitious timing from its point of view, and it will see a victory in prospect. Still, as Charlottetown has shown, things can change, and we will not know until the vote.

---

20 For a discussion of these issues, see "A Ghost at the Banquet: Could Quebec Secede Peacefully? by Kenneth McNaught in *English Canada Speaks Out*, Doubleday Canada, 1992.

But for this book, whether the chances as of today are fifty-fifty or one-in-ten, we assume the referendum passes, as worded by the PQ. And we can only hope the wording will be clear, as Parizeau has promised.

Is a majority enough?

Surely the worst result, for *everyone*, would be a razor-thin affirmative for separation. This would maximize uncertainty as well. Those in ROC wanting to ignore the result would have their reasonable arguments: less than half of the population would have voted for it (depending on the turnout percentage), the anglo minority is being trampled, et cetera.

From the PQ side, the mandate would be less than persuasive, and those who deal from the point of weakness are sometimes less measured and less rational in their approach and negotiations.

It would, in fact, make a lot of sense for someone to attempt to impose a "supermajority" requirement on the existing process—say sixty percent—on two grounds. The first is the very practical one just covered. The second is the principled argument that says fundamental and irreversible change should enjoy overwhelming support. Most constitutions, from countries to clubs, have some such rule.

Alas, who is likely to do so? Surely not the PQ, which has to worry about achieving even fifty percent. And surely not the current government of Quebec, which would show weakness by so doing, and would also face charges of a *prima facie* case of seeking to deny *real* Quebeckers their wish, since everyone knows that a $51/49$ result could only come to pass as a result of an overwhelming pro-separatist sentiment among *francophones*.

The federal government faces the same sort of problem. If we were designing the BNA Act today, we would no doubt require this kind of rule in some euphemistic way, even if it did not directly address the possibility of separation. If Ottawa were to try to move the working majority goalposts today via a proposed constitutional amendment, would this simply infuriate Quebeckers and be counterproductive? Perhaps—but it would be a risk I would recommend. The position has the virtue of distinct fairness and common sense in an otherwise confusing sea of propositions. Unusual change should not be made without an unusual majority. This is a sound view that might appeal to most. But Ottawa may not have this kind of decisiveness and strength.

So even at $51/49$ in the referendum vote, we have a "launch" which will work for the PQ. (There is probably some number—say 50 percent plus one—where this wouldn't fly.) Assuming a launch, then what?

The day after an affirmative referendum, everything will look the same in law. Indeed, unless he renounces his status as a Member of Parliament, Lucien Bouchard will continue to draw his cheque every pay period. Widgets will continue to freely cross provincial boundaries, and chickens and milk will not, as is the case today. Ontario seniors will be free to move to B.C. to do their thing; Ontario lawyers will not. Nothing will have changed—in law.

But everything will have changed—in fact. We will be entering into a period of chaos on both sides of the Ottawa River. While daily life—purchasing groceries, showing up for work—will go on, many longer term things like buying a house, or even a car, will stop until the new realities are worked out. In the economy, everything from the dollar to the debt will be in question.

The challenge, then, will be to respond as quickly and rationally as possible to minimize losses and capture upsides (which do exist). The challenge *today* is to plan for those things.

And so, as important or interesting as all the above issues may be, they are but a prologue if the referendum passes. The legacies that will then be important will not be the arguments pro and con, but the memories of fair play and respect, or otherwise, that each side brings to a consideration of the future. This question of attitudes and referendum tactics will deeply affect the days to come. We will have to be careful, every day.

Chapter 3: First Things First—the Transition

O N THE DAY AFTER THE PASSAGE of a referendum affirming Quebec independence, a number of principal actors will have much to think about. Put yourself in these positions:

Quebec City

You are the Parti Québécois premier, as anglos have always insisted on calling the prime minister of Quebec.[21] Your referendum in favour of separation of Quebec from ROC has just passed. There is jubilation in your party. You and your colleagues are more sober. You know the hard part has now begun, especially if the vote was close.

Parliament Hill

You are the prime minister of Canada. Getting here was the culmination of a life's work. You were elected, in part, because you are a francophone Quebecker. You have fought the fight of your life to defeat the referen-

---

21 This claimed distinction between "premier" and "premier ministre" is not a whim. The former term implies a juniority, and therefore a theory of confederation, that Quebeckers have been unwilling to accept. A few anglophone premiers have seen this clearly as well, and styled themselves "prime minister." Anglophones historically have not bought this usage, and it is one of those cases where language tells a lot about real life.

dum. You have always believed in the Canadian system such as it has been up until now. You have shared that belief along with most others in the country. And now the people of your own province have voted to say goodbye. Of course, you call a Cabinet meeting. But what do you say?

Toronto, Victoria, and other capitals

You are a premier who, save Clyde Wells and Roy Romanow, does not really delight in the constitution of Canada. But you also know this issue is going to take up most of your life for the next year, if not longer, with an opportunity for the history books on the one hand, and ample room to make terrible errors on the other. You call a Cabinet meeting too. Fortunately for you, the press doesn't expect any fast answers.

Ottawa

You are the Governor of the Bank of Canada. You have been talking about this day with your colleagues for months, saying nothing to outsiders, and your exchange rate contingency plan, agreed to with other central bankers, is in place. Will it hold? Will Mr. Chrétien and Mr. Parizeau say what they have agreed to say?

Elsewhere

You are an ordinary citizen, whether postal clerk or bank president. Will you be making any long term moves planning your life in Canada? Not today!

If you have any money to send to the United States, will you do it? Maybe—or maybe not, at this day's exchange rates. And, of course, maybe you can't. Maybe the Canadian dollar is no longer a freely convertible currency on official markets, for an unspecified period of time.

Essential and immediate statements

In the general confusion, there are some obvious things that a number of people have to do at once. These things are obvious because they are in the interest of *everyone*. The key actor on Day 1 is the prime minister of Quebec (as he or she henceforth will certainly be known).

The prime minister of Quebec will have to say (or reaffirm, as these things will have probably been stated during the referendum campaign):

1. The property of foreigners is secure. Assets located inside Quebec, and owned outside, will remain private property, under laws identical in all important respects to those of today.

2. The joint obligations of Quebec and the rest of Canada *vis-à-vis* foreigners will be honoured by Quebec. In particular, Quebec will pay its proper share of the national debt owed to foreigners. The details will be worked out, but anyone registering in such and such a way and in such and such a time (and the details here are very important) will be paid as to "X" percent by Quebec.[22] Moreover, the payment will be in Canadian dollars (which is the currency of almost all federal debt), as long as ROC does not destroy the ability of Quebec to do so.

3. The entire legal structure applicable to Quebec, including federal laws such as the criminal code, will be adopted by the new country, and will only be changed according to normal democratic process.

4. Quebec will honour all treaties entered into by the former Canada, as they apply to the new country of Quebec, especially NAFTA, GATT, and NORAD.

5. There will be no new border controls now or in the future regarding capital, goods, or persons (other than security mat-

---

22 The current PQ position is that Quebec will not accept responsibility for the principal nor make direct payments, sending to Ottawa cheques for interest only on its share of the debt. As this structure is clearly unsatisfactory to ROC (even the share of the debt has not been agreed to), negotiations will be required if there is to be a deal. Moreover, if these negotiations are left until a financial crisis is upon us, the situation will become very confusing and costly, so they should be started now, on a contingency basis, and through back channels to avoid embarrassing publicity for either party, which would simply kill the talks, to our mutual great expense.

ters) entering Quebec from the former Canada, or exiting Quebec to any place wheresoever. Existing border controls (marketing boards, professionals) will continue until otherwise agreed, in the interests of all concerned.

The next important actor is the prime minister of Canada, who one way or another will have to say:

1. We (whoever "we" is at that point) will protect the interests of all of those who elected us. We will define what this means over the next few days.

2. In the meantime, we will absolutely protect the interests of outsiders in this situation. Anyone who has relied upon the word of Canada in financial or other terms will be made whole, whatever unfolds inside our borders.

3. We will now consult all Canadians in this regard.

Next, the Governor of the Bank of Canada will have to say:

1. The prime minister of Canada and the prime minister of Quebec have stated that the commitments of Canada to outsiders are sacrosanct. We will ensure from our point of view that this is true.

The remaining premiers will have to say:

1. So far, we agree.

Our debt trap

Why all of this? Why the emphasis on outsiders, who have no votes?

The very simple reason is that they have the only votes that count on Day 1 after the referendum, which is to say votes-with-your-feet. Foreign money can move—or fail to arrive—on Day 2. You and I do not have that choice, and so, in the short run, we are not players.

Not players in our own country, on this most important day of days? How can this be?

Well, you really have to speak to the former prime ministers about the politics of this, going back at least to John Diefenbaker. They are all responsible to some degree as a result of their handling of the national unity issue, but we shall have no time for that on Day 1. The high court of history and richly-deserved hanging party will have to be organized later.

For our part, we shall have to grapple with the Trudeau/Mulroney economic legacy (little opposed at the time by ourselves as voters, of course) that we are, per capita, one of the most seriously internally indebted nations in the industrialized world, and the absolute champion in per capita debt to foreigners. The practical effect is that we currently require roughly $70 million per day in foreign cash transfusions to prop up our habit and addiction.

Now this is a serious number. It is the negative balance on our current account, where we run a surplus on goods but a huge deficit on services, especially interest on foreign debt. Of course, if the interest isn't paid, the principal will be demanded, and that gets really tough.

So, we will want to avoid having this money cut off right away. (It will have to be very much reduced over time, however.) The price we will have to pay for a continued credit rating will be some reassurance to foreign creditors from the major players. Delivering on these reassurances, if it comes to that, may hurt, but the alternative is painful too. This is a very serious question and people will be making very serious calculations on the costs and benefits of default.

So there is the first element of a successful transition—a joint and several commitment of intent to outsiders by *all* governments in Canada to scrupulously honour all obligations to the outside world.

Maintaining internal stability

The next item is for all governments to agree that no intergovernmental arrangements of any kind will be changed for a breathing period—say six months to a year—while we all consider what next to do. This is certainly a longer period than Quebec would wish, but it is very much in their interest that the rest of us take the time to act in a measured fashion.

So the first matter is to secure and nail down the internal and external status quo, at least temporarily. This will take some fortitude to maintain, because some will test this forbearance. Native groups may mount occupations or other manifestations in Quebec to draw attention to their situation in respect to financial reliance on the federal government, and to call for the redrawing of Quebec's borders. Separatists-in-a-hurry might refuse to pay federal tax, or might ignore other federal laws. It is essential that both jurisdictions enforce the status quo during this period, no matter how cherished the cause of those who would break it. This is terribly important. The avoidance of chaos and violence in separation situations has been extremely rare in this world. It can only be done if order is maintained and emotions kept under control.

The next task is for ROC to decide if it is prepared to live by the results of the referendum. The possible answers are yes, no, or maybe . . . the latter implying something like the Plan C that closes this book. We will return to "yes" or "maybe" in a moment. First a brief consideration of "no!"

Saying "No!"

The consideration of just plain "No!" is brief, because the answer is unlikely—but that certainly doesn't mean it is impossible. Indeed, there will be much early sentiment to look for a way to say "no," and to make it stick. Soft options in trying to make a "No!" answer stick include Ottawa calling a national election on the issue or a national referendum. More of the hard option below.

Calling a national election on the issue of whether or not Quebec should be allowed to separate would hardly return a single supporter of the government from within Quebec, except from a few anglophone ridings. Remember, the issue inside Quebec would not be *should* the province separate—a very specific referendum would have just said "yes" on that issue. Rather the question would be should Quebec be *allowed* to do so. To pose the question is to make clear how a self-respecting electorate would answer.

The main purpose—if any—of a federal election at this point would be either for the current government to receive a mandate from ROC to negotiate or to give some other team an opportunity at that task. That would be dangerous for a government with its prime minister and two top lieutenants from Quebec, and this is not to question their loyalty to Canada. It is a problem of perception, to which Prime Minister Chrétien has already responded with some understandable anger—but the perception exists. The danger for the government would be that the other current main team in Parliament, the Reform Party, might make a case that they would be better at negotiating with Quebec, not having had any part in causing the problem and unburdened with any baggage from Quebec in terms of personnel and loves or hates.

A national referendum held by Ottawa will be a strategy worth considering. It could, for example, ask all Canadians whether they wanted to go the last mile in finding a way to keep the country together. This approach would allow Ottawa to choose the timing, pick the precise question, and orchestrate powerful psychological pressures against Quebec from ROC and from abroad. With this ability, Ottawa could go the good cop or bad cop route. The good cop would hold out a positive vision of a renewed federation. (Unhappily, this has been used before and would be hard to believe.) The bad cop could arrange a scare in interest rates or the marketability of Quebec bonds, arrange for aggressive statements by friendly U.S. Congressmen, and so on, to create a persuasive climate of fear. And if one were to believe that a militant ROC, waving trade and other threats, would be the best weapon against a wavering separatist voter in Quebec, this might be the best way to go. A national referendum campaign might whip up such sentiments. But there are problems and risks.

First is the obvious strategic reply of the Quebec government, which is: "This decision is ours to make, and no one else's. We have made (or will make)[23] our own decision in our own time, in our own way, and to be pressured by Ottawa in this regard is offensive and unacceptable. We will not attempt to prevent the holding of this illegitimate vote in Quebec, but we do urge every good Quebecker to boycott it." There is a good chance that the turnout could be kept low enough that the results of the Quebec referendum, whether held before or after, would have more legitimacy than the federal version.

---

23   In theory, the federal government could hold its own referendum either *before or after* the referendum of the PQ government. However, doing this *before* would be a high-risk strategy, and would not have solved anything if Quebec successfully achieved its own independence vote later.

The second obvious risk is that were such a federal gambit to *fail*, the climate would be well and truly poisoned. An atmosphere of high emotion—even irrationality—would have been cultivated in ROC, which would be exacerbated by a referendum loss and make sensible negotiation difficult for the ROC side. Some might say, "So what?" But if this country *does* break up, our children will live with the consequences of *how* that happened for a very long time. We should not let our understandable emotions cripple their future.

The third and not-so-obvious risk is that parts of ROC might reject a national referendum designed to keep Quebec in Canada. How could this be? Through the formation of some unusual and informal alliances for the immediate purpose, it could be possible. One group in the alliance would be those who are thoroughly fed up with the strain that this constant preoccupation with Quebec has put on proceeding with our lives. This case was very well and respectably put by University of Calgary professors David Bercuson and Barry Cooper in *Deconfederation*.[24] Some of this group are cool and rational, like these authors; others are just plain angry, but they will vote the same way. These people broadly want to keep Canada like it is, and if Quebec is making that impossible, it must go.

The other group in the alliance would have a very different motive, namely a perspective that says that Canada at present is really not working well at all, and that this is a golden opportunity to fix it in important ways, without Quebec to bother us. This includes westerners in particular, some of whom were denied their Triple-E Senate, some of whom remember the National Energy Policy, some of whom are fed up with federal administration of the fishery, or the railroads, or the ports, or the banks. The same group includes, as a much less militant element, decentralists in all parts of Canada, who believe that the general trend to decentralization in the private sector should extend to the public's business as well.

This is not a theoretical risk. Polling results show that even today, before people become *really* mad at Quebec, over 20 percent of voters

---

24   Key Porter Books, Toronto, 1991.

expressing an opinion in ROC say they would favour Quebec separating.[25] (The same poll showed 44 percent of Quebeckers favouring separation, and 51 percent opposed.)

So there is a double risk here: a national referendum might not do well in parts of ROC, especially the west, and it might also give rise to serious questions about the present shape of Canada. Of course, the latter development is inevitable in any case if Quebec leaves.

And, of course, unless a national referendum were to receive some sort of "we want to stay in the current Canada" answer from Quebec, it presumably wouldn't meet the purposes of the federal government in any event. That would be a real challenge, in the circumstances.

(A referendum that posed the question, "Would you like to stay in a very different sort of Canada, that would look precisely like this, as agreed by a Constituent Assembly"—and asked it with equal honesty and equal win/lose consequences to all parts of the country—would be a very different animal that might succeed. This is the business of the final chapter, "Plan C.")

And if neither a national election nor a referendum will work for Ottawa, then saying "No!" in these circumstances really means saying we won't cooperate in allowing Quebec to achieve independent status, and, in fact, we will offer some greater or lesser degree of resistance. That is the hard option that we will be left with, if the soft options don't work.

We then arrive at the Unilateral Declaration of Independence scenario (UDI—another acronym that may become more familiar, if less loved), wherein Quebeckers are told by their provincial government to stop sending taxes to Ottawa, federal public servants in Quebec are invited to continue their existing functions (including military units) under new management, and so on. Francophone Quebec, like white Rhodesia in Africa so long ago, would simply cut the ties, assume the powers, and carry on.

---

25   The Gallup Poll, May 5, 1994. The previously-cited Angus Reid survey found 25 percent of ROC thought it would be "better in the long run if Quebec were simply to separate from the rest of Canada." Thirteen percent supported this strongly; 12 percent moderately.

(We all know what happened to white Rhodesia. Had the secession-ists been the black majority, rather than the privileged white minority, things would have been quite different, in terms of international accep-tance, sanctions, and so on. It is instructive to recall that only a genera-tion ago, the rich anglos of Westmount were then referred to as the "White Rhodesians" of Quebec. Their time has gone.)

UDI is a possible outcome, but one so full of conflict, so disorderly, so wasteful, so unpredictable—so *un-Canadian*, to use an old word—that it does seem unlikely, however many sabres are rattled pre-referendum. If it happens, it happens, and we will get involved in trying to forecast chaos, briefly, in Appendix I.

Saying "Yes!"

Returning to the mainstream, saying "Yes, we accept the referendum result and will negotiate your independence" leads us down the "Plan B" road, with a guaranteed minimum of two countries where one used to be, and a lot of restructuring for ROC.

Saying "Maybe" involves going back to Quebec with a hardline stick and a very sweet carrot—a restructured and highly decentralized Canada that most Quebec separatists could prefer to independence. But this "Plan C" would involve such a change in political thinking for ROC that it is best considered after properly weighing the exigencies of "Plan B." The "least bad" option only gets a good look after the first choices are reluctantly abandoned. (Of course some would even today consider a "Plan C" the best route, but they are few.)

Working through "Plan B" is clearly a two-track affair. One track is a *breakup* process—putting together the negotiating team and conduct-ing the negotiations that will end up with a separate Quebec. The other is a *reconstituting* process—putting together the machinery to decide what ROC should look like in the future. Of the two, the latter track is clearly the far more important one to ROC. The exact composition of any deal with Quebec is really quite marginal to our future comfort, compared to the deal for the future of that part of Canada where we actually live. We have to stop acting as if Quebec were the only question, and we examine that in detail in Chapters 6 and 8. For now, as we talk about the transition, the focus remains on *la belle province*.

The breakup side of the process will be technically complex, emotional, and full of potential flash points. And when it is done, the people on the ROC side of the table will have to be able to *deliver*. (One assumes that capability on the Quebec side because of the two mandates they will have just received.) The problem is that no entity or group of entities in ROC has any kind of mandate whatsoever to negotiate the breakup of Canada. That mandating would have to be the first step. How would it be done?

The simplest way would be to have the existing Parliament of Canada alone give the necessary instructions to the government, or to some specially set up negotiating group. Immediate problems arise. Do Bloc Quebecois MPs have a vote in this process? Do *any* MPs from Quebec? And is a partial Parliament the authentic voice of ROC for this purpose?

Answering this is a political judgement call. My own guess is that any current government that simply proceeded with no more basis than a mandate by a Parliament clearly not elected for the purpose would have serious trouble. It just might have its negotiated deal honoured by ROC, rather than negotiate all over again. But its credibility and its members who participated on this basis would be destroyed forever in the ongoing political business of ROC, whatever that might be.

Far more likely though, such a less-than-credible negotiating team would have a lot of trouble getting anyone to believe it could deliver on a negotiated deal. That would make it a weak negotiator from a mandate point of view, which might suit the other side tactically in the sense of being able to push it around, but would waste time. None of us will have any time to waste in these circumstances.

The government could resign as previously mentioned, and call a new election to select new people to handle the crisis. We immediately encounter some confusion here. Do candidates run from Quebec? Remember, we are at this point still legally one country, and the law provides for Quebec members. Moreover, some percentage of Quebeckers (say, 45, to choose an illustrative number) would *not* have favoured the independence vote. Don't they deserve some kind of representation? Would the new Parliament immediately simply expel all those elected from Quebec, an action which would certainly have the support of the government of Quebec, as long as those MPs were not separatist. Would it simply expel *separatist* MPs from Quebec, who may or may not have run depending on the situation. (Recall that Lucien Bouchard has threatened Parliamentary paralysis if a government refuses to negotiate after a successful referendum vote.) Strong stuff indeed, but remember our assumption: ROC has decided to negotiate separation and is now getting about that work.

In addition, the existing or a new federal government could enlist the aid of the provinces to strengthen credibility. A First Minister's meeting—which would surely have to be called in any case—could mandate a joint federal-provincial committee to negotiate with Quebec and report back to Parliament and the Legislatures. This would provide a lot more political cover than would unilateral action by Ottawa. This is important, because we are going to need all of the political legitimacy in our institutions that we can muster.

This chapter is about process; we will consider the bargaining itself later on. For now, what is clear is that the machinery will have to be set up, and that it should be as broadly mandated as possible, which means including the provinces.

Is that enough legitimacy for this tough negotiating job? For this topic it probably is, though certainly not for the larger *reconstituting* issue. Should more legitimacy be required, federal and provincial governments might wisely include opposition members in the (necessarily small) body governing the negotiators, prior to ratification. We will need all of the wisdom that we can get working on this problem, and so few of these people have given a lot of thought to these issues. This is no disrespect: remember, almost no politicians have. It literally hasn't been allowed.

Ratifying a deal with Quebec

The ratification of any deal once again might conceivably be handled by Parliament only, but that would be unwise. The legislatures should at least be included, with some agreed version of the seven and fifty rule that we are used to in ordinary constitutional change.

What about a referendum on the deal throughout ROC? Again, this is a political call. It would be highly desirable in principle, not just in democratic terms, but also in terms of the psychology of all parties feeling better about getting on with their lives if they have had a voice in the result. So it would be the better thing to do. But—what if it were to fail? Discussions would have to be started all over again with a new group, or, alternatively, the wheels might fall off with no further movement, probably triggering UDI at that point, and leaving a totally disorganized ROC to deal with it.

So, the issue of a referendum to validate a deal, beyond any authority given by Parliament and Legislatures, is not an easy one, as the Charlottetown Accord architects found in less dangerous circumstances. The question will have to be considered in the political climate of the day, and any politicians denying such a vote may simply have to decide to sacrifice their own careers on the altar of getting this thing behind us.

Once again, and as usual in Canada, almost all of the above has been concerned with answering the issues raised by Quebec. (This is to be expected as they have been raising the constitutional issues. Where others had been the squeaky wheels, they have also received the attention, as the Atlantic provinces and, occasionally, wheat farmers on the Prairies have done in other ways.) So, let us say that we establish our negotiating machinery to our general satisfaction and get on with that work, ending up with a deal. Very nice—or at least very definitive—for Quebec. But what about ROC?

Policy vacuum

That is the astonishing vacuum in our politics today. There seems to be an unspoken assumption that if Quebec goes away, the rest of us will carry on in the same old fashion. We will simply carve 75 MPs and 24 Senators out of Parliament, 1,540,000 square kilometres out of the map of Canada, and life will go on. Well, maybe. But let's think about this a bit.

Let's talk first about the glue that holds Canada together today. Some will want to note the shared history on the northern part of this continent. Some will harken back to service in two World Wars. Some will talk about "Hockey Night in Canada" or Pierre Berton or the CPR. This is about a shared culture, and it exists.

Not many will talk about geography, for Canada has been a country in spite of the natural patterns shaped by that force. A few will talk about the desirability of remaining separate from the United States, and this has truly been a defining quantity in our national life. It is unlikely we would have today only one country north of the border were there three or four nations south of that line. Our identity is, in part, a reaction to the Americans.

Not many will talk about economics, for our economics are most unnatural. John A. Macdonald's National Policy and the inter-provincial trade barriers have squeezed us into a shape that works, though it would not be the first choice of most people outside of Ontario.

Some will talk about bilingualism and biculturalism, but they would (in my view) be wrong. Canada has somehow survived *in spite* of those things. It *is* a national characteristic, yes, but not a unifying one.

Some will adduce social programs, above all Medicare. They will be partly right. A distinguishing characteristic of Canadians is our collective sense of wanting to be looked after, and therefore being prepared to look after others. But that in itself says nothing—Alberta or Quebec, each totally alone as a nation-state, could and, no doubt, would carry on some version of Medicare and indeed most social policy, though with different ways and means.

Some will mention economic efficiency. For example, University of British Columbia professors Michael Goldberg and Maurice Levi make the case that Canada considered as an investment vehicle—a "portfolio" of provinces with their different strengths and vulnerabilities—is close to an optimum mix in the portfolio theory sense, and would be weakened by the loss of any significant part.[26] We will return to this in considering the optimum arrangement for the surviving ROC—for any Quebec separation will amount to a rejection of this kind of economic efficiency argument as far as that province is concerned.

Some will mention the Charter of Rights and Freedoms. This has become an unusually important concept in the minds of Canadians in

---

26   "Growing Together or Apart: The Risks and Returns of Alternative Constitutions of Canada," unpublished paper, September 1993.

a very short period of time, which probably says as much about our trust in governments (or lack thereof) and the cult of unbridled individualism blowing about the western world as it says about anything else— though idealism-as-glue is clearly important in some countries. In any case, one can have a Charter in a Canada united as one country, or one can have a Canada separated into ten provinces with Charters of their own. This is not a case for unity, unless you don't trust smaller government.

When you get through the list, it becomes clear that the main glue holding Canada together is that most usual of human characteristics: inertia.

Inertia-as-glue is not a product of the space age. It dates from the beginning of time, like gravity, and is almost as powerful in human affairs as it is in nature. As a glue, however, it doesn't have a lot of stretch and give. It isn't like, say, patriotism or enthusiasm or nationalism, that overlooks all kinds of real problems and stresses and tugs to say, "We are going to be a country anyway!" (These ideals will be the glue of the new Quebec, if it works.) But those kinds of glue lack something in proven durability, too. Say what you like about inertia, but it is long lasting! (as long as it isn't hit by something else).

The best glue for human institutions found to date is shared beliefs. The United States—by far the oldest democracy—shares this characteristic with the older religions, and, in particular, the Roman Catholic church. They all have their catechisms—"I pledge allegiance to the flag" is a temporal example—and they all flex as required to maintain their ideals.

We have been extremely diffident toward such matters in Canada, even declining the opportunity to build up national symbols or heros. Our head of state, the Queen, is a foreigner, and that suits us just fine. We don't glorify one language, or one culture, or one religion, and we manage to see everyone's point of view to the extent where concepts of right and wrong melt and dissolve into a confused political correctitude.

There are some very good things about this laid-back tolerance— indeed, it is one of the finest attributes of Canada. But there is a problem. People who are not determined and passionate about anything less abstract than democracy and motherhood can get taken to the cleaners by more focused elements with more specific goals. People who are tolerant of just about anything are easily divided when inertial patterns are broken.

Timelines

So here we are, ready to negotiate, ready to think about the future of ROC. How long has this taken?

The Quebec election is, say,	Mid-September, 1994
The referendum is, say,	June 24, 1995 (the Quebec national holiday)
The stabilization and negotiation period is agreed at, say,	one year, bringing us to a conclusion on June 24, 1996

This is not very long for such a complex thing as we will be working on in these circumstances. At the same time, uncertainty is dreadfully costly to us all, and we won't want to lag. But either party has the means to delay considerably; they can only shorten the process by agreement (or UDI). So a prolongation of the pain seems the most likely.

In any event, here is where we are at the end of this chapter: the separation referendum has passed, the situation has briefly stabilized, and it is time to get on with whatever comes next.

Chapter 4: The Major Questions for ROC

"To be or not to be . . . that is the question."
—William Shakespeare

QUITE SO. THAT IS THE QUESTION for ROC. What will we want to do in the new circumstances if Quebec goes? And, more basically, who are "we"? Hamlet first proposed this question on stage June 9, 1594. Things went downhill for him for the rest of the play. Perhaps the very act of asking hints at the likely answer.

Does "English Canada" really exist?

There has been little thought given to this question in our unity context, perhaps because it is so painful, or even in some sense "disloyal" to Canada. Those who have canvassed the issue, such as Bercuson and Cooper in *Deconfederation*, unquestioningly conclude that ROC will—and will want to—stay together.

In their brief chapter on "Canada without Quebec," the first assumption is that, "after the separation of Quebec, Canadians will indeed want to maintain Canada. It is our belief that economic self-interest, a common historical experience, and emotional ties to the idea of building a unique North American liberal democracy will lead most Canadians to want to keep Canada, despite its new circumstances, much as it is now. We also think that the prospects of building a more united country based on common political and social values will, in fact, appeal to Canadians."

They go on to say that ROC will welcome the opportunity to address the many economic and social matters we have perforce had to set aside due to our former preoccupation with Quebec. That begun, "we can also turn our attention to the more universal issues that the twenty-first century will force us to address—tradeoffs between economic development and environmental degradation, economic integration, the need for a national educational strategy, the challenge of a world market, the world communications revolutions, and so on."

Well, maybe. We should note their views with care, especially since Bercuson and Cooper hail from Alberta, from which province (British Columbia as well) such residual pan-Canadian thinking is *least* to be expected. This presumably springs from their view that ROC would be based on what they say are "common political and social values."

But my own guess is that the continuity of ROC is very much an open question, since, as I shall argue, it is not a monolithic unit. Certainly the issue will, at a minimum, keep us busy for a year or two, while the rest of the world deals with other cosmic matters.

While Philip Resnick in his *Thinking English Canada*[27] has a different approach, he also believes that something called "English Canada" exists, and will have a continuing will to do so. Resnick finds three viable "nations" in Canada: Quebec, aboriginals, and English Canada. (He is careful to define this latter group to include ethnic and language groups beyond Anglo-Saxon—indeed, he includes all non-French non-aboriginal Canadians in this very large grab-bag.) The major part of his book makes the case for a wakening of "English Canada," in order to begin the discussion of a sort of three-nation arrangement that would keep the country together, yet leave the constituent parts free to realize their destinies. In his much shorter forecast or analysis of alternative futures, he does briefly canvass the possibility of Canada breaking up, but, like Bercuson and Cooper, spends virtually no time on the possibility that what we are calling ROC would itself break up.

---

27   Stoddart Publishing, Toronto, 1994.

If asked to quickly react to that question, most people would agree: if Quebec goes, it would be very unfortunate, but of course the rest of us would carry on together. Ten years ago, the quick-reaction agreement would have been virtually unanimous. Today, cracks are appearing, especially in the west. (In British Columbia, where Premier W.A.C. Bennett once said, "After the last province has left Confederation we will still be there," the Letters to the Editor columns are increasingly sporting local separatist sentiments.)

The ties that bind

To help think about this, let us consider: what are the things that have held Canada together over the years? We have various motives pulling us together and apart, which I will describe as "Because of," "In spite of," and "Rather Than." Here is a list:

Because of :

- Inertia
- History (external and "nation-building")
- National commerce
- Family ties
- Culture (Canadian)
- Federalism (in theory)
- Debt (the joy of incurring)
- Language (alleged)
- Collective/individual rights balance
- Mutual support mechanisms across regions

In spite of:

- Economics
- Geography
- History (internal tensions)
- National commerce (restraint of trade, internal and external)
- Culture (United States)
- Federalism (as practised)
- Debt (the burden of servicing)

- Language (in fact)

Rather than:

- United States (which we don't want to be or join)
- Yugoslavia (a possibility which we fear)
- Bankruptcy (if we split)

One must go beyond some of the bare words to get the full feeling. For example, the elements of "history" and "family ties" gather in the life experiences and friendships of millions of Canadians, crossing provincial boundaries from one part of the country to another. These things exist as simple background in ordinary times, part of the furniture. But scratch a Canadian and tell them their history or family or friends may soon be in another country, and you will rouse some large emotions. The Canada of the political scientist is a foreign country to most of us. Our Canada includes our personal associations.

And, "Our Canada includes Quebec!" as the saying goes. A great many Canadians say and believe this, usually quite unable to articulate why, and not really caring why. That is just their view, a part of their history. Yet at the same time, "our Canada" for many of us seems to include Quebec only if it behaves the way we want them to. Fortunately, there is no law that says people have to be logical. So emotion is one thing, and it is important.

National commerce is also important. To give the largest back-and-forth example, Ontario and Quebec sell each other more than $20 billion per year in goods and services. The most recent Statscan data gave a total for trade in goods and services among Canada's provinces and territories of $146 billion in 1989.[28] In other words, around one dollar in four of this country's production moves as interprovincial commerce. While this is not always appreciated—Toronto in particular is seen to profit from its central role in this—it clearly illustrates how the habits we have gotten into weave us together.

---

28   *The Daily*, August 24, 1993.

But viewed another way, many of these relationships are really a part of the glue of inertia, in the sense that they are determined as a part of a traditional pattern rather than the forces of today. So let us revisit inertia. It is surely the most powerful determinant in human affairs. As a force for continuity, it has great strength. It prevails almost everywhere, almost always. And it is not a bad glue, for two reasons. First, we have learned most of the lessons we know from the past. This is inertia writ large, or conservatism, in political terms.

Second, the surviving elements of a shock will always carry on their course, pulling along any temporary strays, and forcing them back on side, short of a very major shock that destabilizes many main elements of an inertial system. The forces that overcome inertia must be very important—wars, depressions, revolutions, and other dissolutions of the established order. To date, we have never had such a shock in Canada.

But inertia as a glue has another characteristic. It is brittle. It does not easily suffer serious reverses, as say Jewish or native communities or the United States or Switzerland have survived over the years and centuries, in spite of severe tests, based on quite another kind of glue. If the pattern of inertia is broken in Canada, everything will be up for re-examination. What kind of shock could cause this? A Quebec referendum leading to partition of the country would qualify.

The very first question then is, do the residents of ROC (for there is no political organism called ROC) want to reconstitute themselves to change as little as possible, to preserve as much as possible of the past? Or do they want to explore better ways of regrouping?

The answer to this question will have a lot to do with how the topic is to be approached, and what machinery is to be used. Let us first analyze the emotions that will go into the answer, and then the fundamentals.

For a year or so, emotions will get in the way of even posing the question.

If Canada is dealing with a Quebec referendum battle, then during that process, most people in ROC will be concerned only with keeping the country together, subject to one important caveat.[29] In that climate, it is quite impossible to dwell on, or even contemplate, serious differences within the rest of Canada. Otherwise, how can we make a proper presentation to Quebec? Indeed, the marketing, advertising, propaganda, arguments, and pressures of all kinds will be of the sort that will escalate patriotic fervour within ROC.

And after this huge emotional exercise, what happens if the referendum loses? The patriotic attachment to *Canada* will have a momentum of its own, inherited by ROC, carrying beyond referendum day. And yet—if we reach that point—if there were ever a time to suppress that noble patriotic impulse, it would be then.

Patriotism is normally understood to be loyalty to what *is*—but at this point, by our assumption, Canada as we understand it "is" no longer. Loyalty to what *was* is nothing more, nor less, than sentimentality. We shall have to look to the future, not the past.

All this said, the prevailing sentiment the day after a successful referendum in Quebec (from the PQ point of view) may be that the rest of us will now have to stick together more tightly than ever. However, there will also be a sense of failure of what was past, of the old system. This may cause some people, and some of the stronger regions, to wonder if a failed system should be put behind us. It is quite impossible today to forecast which way that sentiment will bounce. As it turns out, other, stronger forces will mean that it does not matter—sentiment will be overwhelmed.

A united ROC

But for now, and based on conventional wisdom, let us take a united ROC as Option 1. We shall get to the other options in Chapter 6. For now, what does this particular new shape of Canada look like?

- There are nine provinces and three territories still left.

---

29   Here is the caveat: this assumes that the federalist referendum campaign is skilfully done. If it is so threatening to Quebec that it is seen to be beyond the pale, or so generous to Quebec that it is seen to set up a second class of citizen in ROC, then patriotic sentiments will be confused by these cross-currents.

- There are 220 MPs and 80 Senators in Ottawa. (To look on the bright side as most Canadians would see it, that means 24 Senators are gone.)
- All laws of general application remain in effect, changed only as required by the absence of Quebec.
- Direct access by land to the Maritimes is cut off. (For those who wish to fight a war about that, please wait for the negotiations. Guaranteed access will surely be part of ROC's bottom line, and one that will be easily ceded.)
- ROC inherits successorship rights to all international ties, rights, and duties. (This is an assumption, not a given, but virtually all observers agree that international organizations would recognize this status. The main imponderable would be which simultaneous successorship rights would also be accorded to the other fragment of the old Canada.)
- All public obligations of ROC to and from Quebec would end at once, or after a defined transition period, except as otherwise negotiated. In practice, this means that governmental cash flows (taxes, transfers, subsidies, et cetera) would cease, and public assets, liabilities, and all other balance sheet items would be frozen. Private payments would continue until stopped by private initiative or new sanctions.
- All public obligations of Quebec to citizens of ROC, and of ROC to citizens of Quebec would continue until changed. This is a horrendously complex skein of relationships, of which the example of public sector employees hired by one jurisdiction and residing in the other is only the most obvious. (And what about, say, that job in the Toronto immigration office, just classified bilingual, filled by the new appointee from Dorval and under appeal by the unilingual incumbent?)

Other questions arise. What about the pensions that are owed by one jurisdiction to residents of the other—not OAP, which will end, being a straight transfer payment, but "earned" rights such as CPP (which of course is not earned, but that is the fiction)—or the pensions of federal or Quebec Public Service retirees?

There will be many such vexing questions, large to those directly concerned, but minor to ROC, for which the big question will be: "Who are we—if we are an ongoing entity at all?"

Let us examine table 4.1 which compares some distributional attributes of Canada and ROC.

Table 4.1: The Makeup of ROC					
	Atlantic Provinces	Ontario	Sask. & Manitoba	Alberta	British Columbia
Population 1994 (millions)	2.391	10.847	2.120	2.681	3.599
Percentage of Canada's population, 1994	8.3%	37.4%	7.3%	9.3%	12.4%
Percentage of ROC's population, 1994	11.0%	49.9%	9.8%	12.3%	16.6%
GDP per capita, 1994 estimate ($)	19,215	27,247	22,401	29,271	27,018
Rank of unit in world economy according to per capita GDP[a]	31	11	20	6	14
Number of Seats in the House of Commons	32	99	28	26	32
Percent of House of Commons seats (CDA)	10.9%	33.6%	9.5%	8.8%	10.9%
Percent of House of Commons Seats (ROC)	14.6%	45.0%	12.7%	11.8%	14.6%
Number of Seats in the Senate	30	24	12	6	6
Percent of Seats in the Senate (CDA)	28.9%	23.1%	11.5%	5.8%	5.8%
Percent of Seats in the Senate (ROC)	37.5%	30.0%	15.0%	7.5%	7.5%

Table 4.1: The Makeup of ROC

	Atlantic Provinces	Ontario	Sask. & Manitoba	Alberta	British Columbia
Distance of unit's capital from Ottawa (km)	1,104	351	1,948	2,844	3,587
Balance of Trade in Goods & Services with ROC, 1989[b] (million $)	-5,868	18,482	-3,913	-2,091	-5,714
Balance of Trade in Goods & Services with Canada, 1989[b] (million $)	-8,205	21,911	-4,240	-2,620	-7,556
Balance of Trade in Goods & Services with Rest of the world, 1989[b] (million $)	28	-9,170	2,150	4,362	5,837
Estimated net transfer from the Federal government[c] to the unit, fiscal year 1990/91 (million $)	8,427	-18,741	2,515	-2,182	-3,878

[a]based on 1992 data.
[b]Only the Balance of Trade in Goods and Services is available since there are no data on transfers by region.
[c]Net transfer is defined as spending net of interest, less taxes.
Sources: *1994 Corpus Almanac and Canadian Sourcebook*; *The Daily*, August 24, 1993, Statistics Canada; *Canadian Economic Observer*, catalogue 11-010, Statistics Canada; *Public Sector Assets and Liabilities*, catalogue 68-508, Statistics Canada, March 1994; *Provincial Outlook*, Spring 1994, Conference Board of Canada, April 14, 1994; *Inside Canada's Government Debt Problem and the Way Out*, Robin Richardson, International Centre for the Study of Public Debt, *Fraser Forum Critical Issues Bulletin*, The Fraser Institute, May 1994; *Government Spending Facts 2*, Isabella Horry and Michael Walker, The Fraser Institue, forthcoming 1994.

Note: Divisions were chosen on the following basis:

• Atlantic is a semi-geographic unit and fully residual region after cut-off.

- Ontario is big enough to be a country.
- Saskatchewan/Manitoba is not big enough to be a country, but could join east or west, depending on willingness and/or invitations.
- Alberta is rich enough to be a country.
- British Columbia is a viable country.
- Here and elsewhere it is assumed that the Territories will connect with one or more of the provinces, so no separate analysis is conducted.

The logic here is this: regions that might like to think of themselves as entities should be analyzed from that point of view as long as it even marginally makes sense. The above listing comprises the main probabilities, save potential nation-state aspirations by Newfoundland or P.E.I., which are possible, but tangential for these purposes. Therefore, with apologies, the Atlantic region is treated as a unit. This deserves further micro-analysis from an Atlantic point of view.

The first thing that becomes apparent is that Ontario, which used to be about 40 percent of Canada, is now 50 percent of ROC. Indeed, Ontario is so large, so wealthy, and so diverse that it could easily be a nation-state on its own.

This raises several questions, as follows.

Politics

Representation by population is a fundamental tenet of our democracy and is not likely to be abandoned. Even under Canada, the way our federal government has actually worked is that most policies are developed from the huge Ontario population perspective, subject to a de facto Quebec veto. In ROC, Ontario would be dominant and constitute almost a clear majority in a federal scheme of things. Would this be acceptable to the West?

At least for now, in what may be a transient or permanent phenomenon, Ontario and the West, especially B.C. and Alberta, have very different majority political philosophies, as represented by the Liberals and by Reform. This is no small thing, no coincidence. This constitutes a "fault line," to use Jeffrey Simpson's phrase, for a nascent political cleavage.

The instinctive Reform position of bridging this fault line and the demographic imbalance with a political structure would be to create a new variant of the "Triple E" Senate. In a 10 seat-per-province (ignoring the Territories for the moment), 90 seat Senate, the West would have 40 seats, the Atlantic the same, and Ontario only 10. (This idea would import the practice of many federations, of which the United States is the most familiar to us, of an Upper House representing regions, wielding very substantial power over the population-based House of Commons.)

But why would Ontario buy this? The downside for Ontario, of course, is that a Triple-E (Elected, Effective, and Equal) Senate of this kind would quickly restructure the balance of power in the country, not just in politics, but in economics and social programs as well, in ways that might be inconvenient to Ontario. See "Economics," below.

However, the real problem with this solution, on reflection, might be for the West. There are two main reasons for this. The first is that the Atlantic would have an inordinate amount of power under such a system, compared to its population or economy. The financial transfers that the region has received in the past through the grace and favour of the governing party of the day would, under the new system, be much escalated, and extracted by raw political power.

The second reason, never really pondered by most Reformers supporting Triple-E, is that the system is inherently centralizing. The regional legitimacy of the United States Senate is what has conferred such enormous and pervasive powers on Washington, D.C. That outcome is quite the opposite of the goal sought by most westerners, which is to proceed with their lives with as little direction as possible from a government based thousands of miles away.

Economics

The historic economics of Canada as they have evolved over 127 years have reduced the Maritimes to client states, and proud Newfoundland to a welfare case. After an initial surge of investment, the arrangements have made no continuing sense for British Columbia and Alberta, the economies of which are consistently and systematically exploited by the taxation and financial structures at the national level. After some measure of success earlier this century, Saskatchewan and Manitoba are again net beneficiaries of the transfer system, but they are not yet so utterly dependent as their eastern cousins. Only for Ontario, and Ottawa, has the Canadian economic system consistently worked well.

With the gradual decline of tariffs and quotas over the past generation, this has started to change. At the same time, based on its vast material, human, and financial infrastructure depth, the Ontario economy is doing a reasonable job of changing, as well, to meet the new times. Many of the old manufacturing industries are dying, but new ones are growing. Under the protective cover of the Canadian system, Ontario appears to be meeting the challenge of NAFTA and other sorts of international competition, albeit with marked assistance from a falling dollar.

In an Ontario-dominated ROC, this state of affairs could be expected to continue. On the other hand, in a Triple-E ROC, as mentioned above, things would change. Without question, a Triple-E central government would take affirmative steps to milk the strengths of Ontario to subsidize the Atlantic and pump up the western economy, wisely or not. This is simply inherent in the observed nature of federal systems of this kind, and there is no point in making plans for ROC based on planned behaviour that is nobler or wiser than others like us have exhibited in the past.

There is nothing wrong with a shift in geographic emphasis on economic activity. What is wrong with this picture is that subsidies would be required to make it happen.

As a tentative conclusion, then, the political quid pro quo necessary for the continued existence of ROC carries the probability of significant economic costs, from this one dimension alone.

Policy matters

What would some of the major policy questions facing a continuing ROC be? One could be certain that at least some of the enduring issues facing Canada would be dealt with in new ways by ROC—were it able to find consensus.

Where the changes are a natural outcome given the departure of Quebec, language for instance, that is simple enough. Where they are the result of a fundamental rethinking of old policies that survive simply because they have been politically correct under the old order, this will be more difficult. Some of the following areas are illustrated below.

Language policy

Bilingualism will clearly end, and quickly, no matter what form ROC takes. English will be the language of ROC and its constituent parts. (New Brunswick, being officially bilingual for good reasons of its own, may continue to be so.)

The subsequent languages of study in the ROC school and business systems will be predominantly Spanish, Cantonese, Mandarin, and Japanese. French will be studied less, not only less than it is today, but indeed for emotional reasons, less than continued commerce with Quebec would justify. This will be a low-cost reaction for ROC, since Quebec will have to do most of its external business in English anyway.

In order for the above to happen, the Official Languages Act will either have to be repealed or ignored. Moreover, and more problematically, that section of the Charter of Rights and Freedoms dealing with the absolute right to an education in either English or French "where numbers warrant" will have to be dealt with. Technically, this is far tougher, and will provide a battlefield for those still clinging to the old ways—in the hope that Quebec might one day "return"—to fight for their cause. Even as simple a thing as this, in other words, will be divisive.

Cultural policy

The federal government, directly and through its emanations, currently spends some $1.3 billion (fiscal 1991) per year on "culture" (not including the CBC), of which perhaps $300 million is spent in Quebec. It contributes a further $1 billion to the CBC budget, mentioned separately because the sum is so large, of which about 29 percent goes to the French network, Radio Canada.

The justification for a federal presence in this area has always been that of "Canadian Unity." By definition, we shall enter into an era where Canada no longer exists. Will there be any disposition whatsoever from the taxpayer to fund these kind of sums, less the Quebec share of course, for "ROC Unity"? It lacks a certain something.

The attitude will no doubt vary throughout ROC. The Toronto area, the largest recipient of such dollars and the locus of ROC's cultural industry, will want the cash flows to continue. Others may feel differently—not so much as to the value of cultural activities per se, but as to whether a central funding mechanism is any longer the right way to go, compared to regional or local taxing and decision-making.

This latter sentiment is anathema to the cultural industry, as it is to many other supplicants to the public purse. It has always been very convenient to have two places to go for public money—just name your worthy cause. If one source flags, the other may prosper, and on occasion they may be played off against each other. Usually the reluctant level of government may be embarrassed into a matching stance at least, once the other is on board. In this sense, culture and some other aspects of our society would be in the same strategic position as the Third World after the end of the Cold War—no one will bid for their favour any more.

Table 4.2: Equalization payments 1992/93 (millions of dollars)	
Newfoundland	$877
P.E.I.	173
N.S.	869
N.B.	1,055
Quebec	3,572
Ontario	0
Manitoba	868
Saskatchewan	531
Alberta	0
B.C.	0
Source: Provincial Government Public Accounts.	

This is something to think about. Duplication has always been marked down as a defect of our federal system, and a very costly one. It also introduces some elements of competition. There are gives and takes, as in most things.

In any event, it is difficult to foresee ROC spending much money on culture for unity reasons, the old "Canadian culture" defence having just failed to save the old country. Local and private funding will be the new reality, whatever form ROC takes.

Equalization and other inter-regional aid

Canada has an incredibly complex web of inter-regional transfers in the public sector. Here are some of the larger:

- Equalization—paid to all provinces except B.C., Alberta, and Ontario. In the latest available year, 1992/93, about $8 billion was paid under this formula, in the distribution shown in table 4.2

  Equalization could be one of the noblest of Canadian concepts, were it devoted strictly to ensuring that all young Canadians, who cannot control where they live, would have an equal start in life. It becomes an important philosophical debate as to whether the concept should be extended further than that, and a bit of a scandal when elements of the pork barrel enter into setting the numbers. As any provincial Finance Minister will tell you, the feds set the results first, and then jigger the extremely complex and flexible formula to make the desired numbers happen for the chosen political objectives.

- Regional Development Subsidies in 1991 were running a bit over $500 million, as table 4.3 indicates.

  If the federal government wants to subsidize regions, it should just give the regions the money. There is absolutely no evidence of

Table 4.3: Federal government spending on Regional Planning and Development Fiscal Year 1990/91 (millions of $)	
Newfoundland	$11
P.E.I.	3
N.S.	21
N.B.	15
Quebec	131
Ontario	240
Manitoba	26
Saskatchewan	9
Alberta	31
B.C.	42
Canada	531

Source: Isabella Horry and Michael Walker, *Government Spending Facts 2*, The Fraser Institute, forthcoming 1994.

great central government wisdom in this regard.

- Distribution of UI and business subsidies across the land in 1992 are shown in table 4.4.

    Once again the major inter-regional transfers are obvious. UI was never conceived as a regional program, but it has become that, par excellence. Once again, if Canadians want to perform this kind of regional transfer, there are more efficient ways of doing so. There is not a provincial government in this country that would disagree with this—as long as the influx of dollars into *its* province wasn't cut.

Table 4.4: Unemployment Insurance Premiums and Benefits by Province, 1992

Province	Unemployment Insurance Premiums	Unemployment Insurance Benefits	Net Inflow to Provinces (Benefits – Premiums)
	(Millions of $)		
Newfoundland	$257	$1,046	$789
P.E.I.	66	207	141
N.S.	514	816	302
N.B.	413	850	437
Quebec	4,300	5,586	1,286
Ontario	7,515	5,189	-2,326
Manitoba	631	482	-149
Saskatchewan	488	387	-101
Alberta	1,734	1,296	-438
B.C.	2,201	2,085	-116
Canada	18,221	18,014	

Source: *Provincial Economic Accounts 1988-1992*, catalogue 13-213, Statistics Canada.

- There are also business subsidies as shown in table 4.5, and they are quite large.

    One wonders why the federal government should be in this area at all. The numbers are blatantly discriminatory by region, and if that is the purpose of the subsidies, it should be stated up front. As for the concept of subsidies to business, no government has much of a record in "picking winners," and a government as far away from the action as Ottawa is certainly the wrong agent for this task.

- In all, the distribution of the entire federal budgetary expenditure across the provinces in the most recently calculated year of 1990 breaks down as shown in table 4.6.

    In interpreting table 4.6, readers are advised to pay special attention to the "Interest" factor on the federal debt. The appro-

Table 4.5: Federal Transfer payments to Business, 1992		
Province	Subsidies	Capital Assistance
	(millions of $)	
Newfoundland	100	185
P.E.I.	53	20
N.S.	124	57
N.B.	220	60
Quebec	986	241
Ontario	1,703	352
Manitoba	416	61
Saskatchewan	906	38
Alberta	756	68
B.C.	338	67
Canada	5,617	1,152

Source: *Provincial Economic Accounts, 1988-1992*, catalogue 13-213, Statistics Canada.

Table 4.6: The Distribution of Federal Government Spending Across the Provinces, 1990

	NFLD	PEI	NS	NB	QUE	ONT	MAN	SASK	ALTA	BC	TERR	CDA
Culture & Recreation	2.8%	1.0%	7.1%	3.7%	21.9%	37.0%	5.1%	3.3%	7.1%	9.8%	1.2%	100.0%
Education	5.3%	1.1%	6.0%	5.6%	25.7%	22.7%	7.7%	6.2%	9.3%	10.1%	0.2%	100.0%
Environment	3.9%	0.8%	3.8%	3.4%	27.6%	33.7%	4.0%	3.7%	8.2%	10.2%	0.4%	100.0%
Foreign Affairs	2.2%	0.5%	3.4%	2.7%	25.4%	36.6%	4.1%	3.7%	9.3%	11.8%	0.3%	100.0%
General Services	2.7%	1.0%	8.1%	3.9%	21.4%	38.5%	4.7%	3.0%	6.5%	9.4%	0.9%	100.0%
Health	3.5%	0.8%	5.4%	4.2%	27.3%	30.1%	5.8%	4.4%	8.0%	9.8%	0.8%	100.0%
Housing	3.4%	1.0%	4.0%	3.8%	22.1%	30.3%	5.2%	9.6%	12.1%	6.7%	1.7%	100.0%
Labour	2.2%	0.7%	6.6%	3.1%	22.0%	39.7%	4.3%	2.8%	7.4%	10.5%	0.6%	100.0%
Other	3.4%	1.0%	6.1%	5.3%	31.3%	30.1%	3.2%	2.8%	7.8%	8.0%	1.0%	100.0%
Interest Payments	1.1%	0.3%	2.6%	1.5%	18.3%	59.8%	2.5%	1.6%	4.4%	7.6%	0.4%	100.0%
Protection	1.9%	0.7%	8.8%	7.4%	19.6%	38.3%	4.7%	1.8%	7.4%	9.0%	0.4%	100.0%
Reg. Planning & Dev't	2.1%	0.5%	4.0%	2.8%	24.8%	45.1%	4.9%	1.8%	5.8%	7.9%	0.3%	100.0%
Resource & Industrial Dev't	2.6%	1.1%	4.1%	2.7%	14.9%	22.4%	7.1%	17.3%	20.0%	6.4%	1.3%	100.0%
Research Establishments	1.9%	0.3%	3.4%	2.6%	24.9%	38.2%	3.6%	3.6%	9.2%	12.1%	0.2%	100.0%
Social Services*	3.9%	0.8%	4.4%	4.0%	28.4%	30.8%	4.1%	3.6%	7.4%	12.3%	0.3%	100.0%
Canada Pension Plan	2.0%	0.5%	4.9%	3.3%	0.4%	52.3%	5.6%	4.9%	9.3%	16.6%	0.1%	100.0%
Transp. & Comm.	4.4%	1.3%	7.4%	5.6%	20.8%	33.0%	4.9%	4.2%	8.6%	8.5%	1.1%	100.0%
Total	**2.7%**	**0.7%**	**4.7%**	**3.6%**	**23.1%**	**40.0%**	**4.1%**	**3.6%**	**7.2%**	**9.7%**	**0.5%**	**100.0%**
Total Net of Interest Payments	**3.2%**	**0.8%**	**5.5%**	**4.4%**	**22.9%**	**33.9%**	**4.8%**	**4.4%**	**8.5%**	**11.1%**	**0.5%**	**100.0%**

*Social Services does not include CPP. Source: *Government Spending Facts 2*, I. Horry and M. Walker, The Fraser Institute, forthcoming 1994.

priate figure to look at is on the very bottom line, showing expenditure by province *not including* federal debt interest paid to bondholders in any given province. This is made obvious by the following thought: if all of these federal bonds were sold to foreigners tomorrow, the pattern of federal expenditures that we really care about would not change. The major share of interest payments currently go to Ontario because that is where the majority of the bonds are held for now, but they could be held anywhere.

As one other complication, please note that Quebec received very material amounts not available to other provinces under a "contracting out" tax point formula, which is not reflected in this table.

Some surprising findings come out of these tables. In particular, it is not surprising that the "have" provinces of B.C., Alberta and Ontario all receive substantially less than their "share," by population, of expenditures. What *is* surprising is that Quebec receives less too. The popular impression that Quebec is a significant beneficiary from the "have" provinces arises, correctly, because Quebec pays an even smaller share of total federal revenue.

Note: when these or any other federal expenditures are paid for by increased debt, the *benefits* are transferred regionally, and that is generally all we watch. Alas, the costs are regionally transferred too, *usually in the other direction*, in a regional sense. This is because the debt will eventually be paid by the richer regions, while the dollars are spent in the poorer regions. The eventual distortion effect where this observation applies therefore must roughly be doubled!

The above are but the most egregious and easily identified regional subsidies and payments. The focus of Export Development Corporation loans, the distortion due to various national marketing board orders preventing inter-provincial competition, the Crow Rate and other regulatory subsidies, footwear and textile trade restrictions—each and every one of these and many others are large dollar items that amount to inter-regional transfers.

Straight talk about paying the bills

After the referendum—or perhaps even before—every Ministry of Finance in every province will have its computers whirring to nail down these sorts of numbers. They will become bullets in the ensuing debate about what a fairly organized ROC would look like.

The dialogue is likely to be rather harsh. This will be the first well-informed, honest, and open talk about winning and losing among ROC's regions that has ever taken place. Tradeoffs of this sort have always been made in the privacy of Cabinet and Caucus and First Minister's meetings. As they say about sausage, if you knew how it was made, you mightn't like it so much. We will find out how equalization is made, for example. (According to many insiders, the last round in early 1994 was clearly rigged to benefit Quebec with some benefit for the Atlantic, while denying any adjustment to the iniquitous capping of social payments to other provinces.)

The federal mindset over the years has been that problems in people's lives, even those of their own making, must be cushioned at all costs. They seem to have assumed that our productivity could afford such a policy, regardless of affordability. Moreover, the policy has been that where regional votes come into play, they must be secured (or bought, as a cynic might say). Every political party has played that game. With the recent squeeze on finances, it is no longer affordable. There is always a lot of finger-pointing at such times. When it is combined with an "everything-up-for-grabs" reassessment time, real sentiments will surface.

Recently, one has started to read comments that British Columbians are not willing to finance Newfoundlanders sitting on a barren rock. Newfoundland fishers are saying they should be paid for exactly that because they are facing nothing more nor less than a crop failure, always subsidized on the Prairies. (The facts are hugely different, but that is not the point.)

One hears about immigrants costing a lot of money, about them being let into the country as a federal decision, with the feds then walking away from the costs. The use of UI in illegitimate ways all across the country by many is taken as an article of faith, but the West broadly thinks that the East is the real villain here. And whenever inter-regional transfers result from distorted trading patterns, the free-trade West has a grievance against Ontario—as indeed does the Atlantic.

When all is summed up, the situation is this: a gradually achieved, delicately balanced regional transfer pattern, rife with inequities but still maintained by inertia, will almost certainly be destabilized by the events contemplated in this book. This is first because one of its largest elements, Quebec, will have been removed, and, second, because it will be closely and openly questioned and weighed for fairness for the first time.

The overall transfer pattern will not pass this test of close scrutiny. The "losers" in this transfer game will for the first time clearly understand who they are and how big the loss is. Some of this understanding will come from governments, and some from private interest groups, but once these rocks are rolled over, the fighting will begin.

Immigration policy

Brief allusion was made above to the federal payment responsibilities for immigration costs. This is important on its own, but shrinks *vis-à-vis* the social and political considerations.

Quebec, with its low growth problem (if it is a problem), has always been pro-immigration, as long as it is francophone. Quebec will be gone.

ROC has been more mixed in its view. Areas such as the Atlantic and Saskatchewan/Manitoba are generally favourable, because they can use any new activity, they are humanitarian, and, of course, they don't receive many immigrants anyway. For example, the total immigrant population in Saskatchewan is 6 percent, and 1.5 percent in Newfoundland.

Toronto and Vancouver have shared a very different experience. The immigrant populations of these two cities as of 1991 was 38 and 30 percent respectively.[30] Each sees a growing backlash on the subject—not so much with respect to immigration per se, but with respect to pace and mix. This constitutes another fault line, above all political, with

---

30   All figures are from Statistics Canada, *Immigration and Citizenship*, and *The Daily*.

Liberals and Reform once again taking opposite sides, broadly as proxies for East and West, old and new, political correctness and populism.

While the generalization may be overly large, the West wants fewer immigrants, more precisely targeted to western needs for employment and Pacific Rim skills. The eastern part of ROC seems broadly content with approximately the same number and mix of immigrants, with a major emphasis on humanitarianism and family reunification (with its attendant electoral benefits).

Mobility

In a sense, this is an upside-down issue, and the obverse of the regional-transfers coin. It is only slight exaggeration to say that those west of the Ottawa River believe in the mobility of Canadians, both in theory and in practice. The prevailing ethic is that people not only should have the *option* of mobility, but they should be subject to pressures in that direction.

As a province, Quebec has never believed in this theory for linguistic and cultural reasons: mobility implies loss of both, and for too large a cost, whatever the economics say. (Of course many Quebeckers *have* moved elsewhere—and they have lost their language and culture.)

People in the Atlantic have been cushioned against the exigencies of mobility, in ways that people in other parts of the country generally think are wrong.

Aboriginal issues

As it was with the Charlottetown Accord, this will be one of the flash points of the debate within ROC. It is one more facet of the political correctness/populism split that informs so much of the dialogue, popping up as well in cultural debates, immigration, and social policy. Views on aboriginal policy are very different across the country; they are also in rapid evolution.

With Quebec gone (and we shall hear an enormous amount about the consequences for natives in that country if Quebec does go), the hardest-line society *vis-à-vis* native questions will have left ROC.[31] That does not mean that all of the serious differences will be gone.

The politically correct position on aboriginals in ROC is that this group collectively forms one or more "nations" in the social and cultural sense, and is entitled to many or most of the attributes of nationhood in a political, nation-state sense. This was the attitude that led to the self-government position in the Charlottetown Accord; this is the view that continues to guide the major governments concerned, in Ottawa, Ontario, and British Columbia.

The Ottawa position is a relatively new one, developed during the Mulroney years, but apparently fully adopted by the Chrétien government. (This is notwithstanding Mr. Chrétien's White Paper of two decades ago, when he was Indian Affairs Minister. This paper essentially provided for natives to become ordinary Canadians.)

The Trudeau-Mulroney era has given some (Canadian) constitutional teeth to the new thinking, as a result of the amendments of 1982. Such elements of the Canadian constitution may or may not survive in whatever becomes of ROC, because ROC or whatever will have a *new* constitution, which may or may not incorporate all of the features of the old one.

The current Ontario and British Columbia positions are of even shorter duration than that of Ottawa, being in effect solely the creatures of new socialist governments that have adopted the third nation, self-government concept holus bolus. Both of these governments are extremely weak and may not survive their next respective elections. Nevertheless, and especially in British Columbia, they are entering into binding "government-to-government" agreements in a growing number of areas, with the clear intention that these agreements should be merged and converted into long-term self-governance and ownership of large parts of the province, with management of even larger areas.

---

31 As a somewhat ironic possible footnote to history, the price of their peaceable departure will almost certainly include an extremely generous settlement with native groups in the province, agreed to as a tactical move to smooth the way to independence.

The actions of all three of these governments are much at variance with the views of the electorate. To oversimplify, perhaps, the more general view is that all necessary resources should be made available to assist with education and other development, that native culture should be respected, that all legal obligations should be scrupulously met, and beyond that, that natives should be ordinary Canadians. Indeed, there is evidence that the proposal to the contrary—a planned "third order of government"—was a very important factor in the general defeat of the Accord at referendum.

As the elements of ROC examine their future, this matter, having been always handled by the central government, will have to be dealt with one way or another. It will not weigh in favour of the continuation of any central government whose aboriginal policy is very much out of sync with that of most of the country. That makes the issue a major question for ROC.

Indeed—and to insert an editorial comment at this point—this is an example of why the "glue" that Ottawa relies on today is mostly mere inertia. In so many basic policy areas, and for so long, the central government has been following policies more and more out of favour in the country. This could be continued with impunity as long as all of the alternatives, all of the other political parties, signed on to the same policies, and in every important policy context, that was true of the Conservatives, Liberals, and NDP.

This arrangement fell apart so dramatically in the election of October 23, 1993, *at the very first opportunity to vote for a real alternative.* The amazing one-election growth of Reform and the Bloc Québécois are without precedent. Only a huge pent-up anti-Ottawa feeling could have prompted this. These same forces have very seriously eroded most lingering feelings of loyalty or generosity to our central authority, and this may prove to be the most enduring legacy of the three old parties.

Trade issues

Trade policy, both internal and external, is an obvious source of difference within ROC. It is quite true that recent liberalization advances in the FTA and then NAFTA have reduced the potential strains as there are simply fewer barriers to fight about. But that does not mean there will be no fights at all. Recall that Quebec was an active champion of NAFTA, while Ontario broadly opposed it—not just the NDP government, but most politicians and the popular press. In a ROC without Quebec, would a dominant Ontario resume its protectionist pressures?

It remains broadly in the interests of the West to move towards full and free trade at once, and it is much against the interests of Ontario interests to do so. Given the schedules of GATT, the progressive reductions of NAFTA, and the fervent wish of those in the agricultural sector everywhere to just hang on to as much of their preference for as long as they can, the stresses on ROC in this area of trade could be large.

The Charter

The Charter of Rights and Freedoms has attained a sort of religious regard in most of ROC, with some pockets of fierce resistance, including provincial governments. (For all the fine words of politicians at the time, the "notwithstanding" clause is considered by governments to be a very necessary protection from unforeseen consequences of the Charter, and never faced any chance whatsoever of removal in the last constitutional round.)

However, post-referendum, the Charter will have to be opened up. There is no alternative because of the language sections. That will open up another huge field for debate and disagreement, the divisions of which will again likely have geographic content.

What we shall be hearing about in a re-opened Charter will be the following difficult issues:

- collective rights versus individual rights
- sexual orientation and the meaning of the family
- property rights

All three of these are very important and deeply emotional, and all have an element of East/West cleavage.

The purpose of this section has been to identify conflicts that ROC would have to address in considering whether to stay together. It is evident that there are enough questions of a serious nature that there will be no foregone conclusion. After debating these matters, ROC might simply carry on as an entity—or it might not. And that will bring consequences.

There is a whole other set of questions that will have to be asked if ROC should wish to consider breaking up: the distribution of the debt, continuation (if any) of equalization as "foreign aid" for some transitional period, ongoing trade policy between units, et cetera. These will be canvassed in the chapter discussing alternative shapes for ROC.

Chapter 5:
Attitudes

C ANADA WAS NOT CONCEIVED in an act of passion, nor has it been maintained at a pitch of patriotic fervour. It would be a mistake to end it that way—with fiery speeches and hot blood flowing. Yet in any time of turmoil, there will be those who will fan the available passions of the moment for their own purposes. This will be a major challenge, a major threat to our ability to properly grapple with the greatest decision in our history.

So this is a chapter about attitudes. As every negotiator knows—indeed, as each of us know from our own lives, many outcomes are possible in most situations. It is no exaggeration to say that how we approach our friends (and non-friends!) in ROC, in Quebec, and in the rest of the world will really determine whether we come through a post-referendum challenge in good shape or bad. But there will be several theories as to what this proper approach is, ranging from total calm through to unremitting bluster. The most important attitudes to discuss will be those inside ROC, but let us put that in the context of our surroundings.

The attitude of the rest of the world will be fairly simple to predict. It will be largely one of indifference, tinged here and there with regret about upheaval in one of the formerly and too rare solid places on the planet. But the rest of the world will be entirely ready to do business with whatever political structures emerge, and they will not be above seeking their own advantage in this process.

For example, where we as a nation have obtained this or that concession or special treatment in the international community, others will seek to take our place. This may relate to membership in the G-7 or to this or that committee of the United Nations, or even to trying to purchase some particularly pleasant embassy building that we can perhaps no longer afford. In short, then, the rest of the world will see this as nothing more than another adjustment and an opportunity in the ongoing Darwinian nature of national states.

United States interests

The attitude of the United States will be one of special importance. There is a disposition in ROC to suppose that the Americans would have a special leaning or sentiment to us, as opposed to Quebec, when the time comes for choices. This is a very foolish supposition. The United States will follow its own advantage, as it should. In particular, we may think they should be helpful to ROC in putting pressure on Quebec, either pre-referendum to pressure the Quebec voter, or post-referendum to make Quebec "pay" for its decision. But why should the United States do this?

First, in the pre-referendum period, the Americans will be studiously neutral, and would be foolish to be anything else. It is not just that it is the proper thing to do in international terms where purely internal questions are under discussion. More than that, why offend either side, when you don't know who will win? There is nothing that Canada can give the United States in appreciation should the "No!" side defeat the referendum. Indeed, obvious American pressure on this side might be counterproductive in Quebec, and might scare the enduring contingent of Yank-haters in ROC.

And the Americans will not be worrying about national security and defence issues. They know, and we know, that they can provide the only serious defence of ROC in any case, and we are not likely to change our disinclination to pay more money to look after this ourselves. And they know, and Quebec knows, that the very first treaty the new Quebec will sign will relate to continental security, and the tight embrace of the American eagle—or else!

But there will be no slavering south of the border to grab the territory of the former Canada. "54-40 or fight" went out as a political slogan in the nineteenth century. The last thing in the world a delicately-balanced United States political system needs is the addition of another dozen Senators with liberal attitudes about medicare and guns and other dangerous ideas. The United States will remain quite content to take our resources and our investment opportunities, as always, and leave us to our other pursuits as long as their defence interest is secured.

One knows perfectly well, however, that books will be written, and sold, about how the Americans are plotting to drain our water and other things, and take over our real estate if there is any trouble. May those authors prosper. If the Americans want to do such things, the combined might of the Quebec and ROC armies times ten won't make a whole lot of difference.

While the disappearance from some international forums of Canada as an ally would be a downside in terms of other U.S. geopolitical interests, it would open avenues to reward other friendly and ambitious nations with the vacated positions, so this is largely a wash.

As to the situation post-referendum, there are many things about the United States trading relationship with Canada that they consider irritants, but have reluctantly accepted. Cultural industries and supply-managed agriculture (marketing boards) are two major cases in point. Let us consider supply management first.

ROC hugely subsidizes the Quebec dairy industry, in terms of so-called industrial milk, through both quotas and payments.[32] This would naturally stop, post-separation. Quebec will then naturally attempt to cushion its dairy farmers (who hold a lot of votes) with an ongoing subsidy of its own. This would run counter to GATT, and ROC would probably argue that there is no reason why it or the Americans

---

32 According to the *Agricultural Policies, Markets, and Trade Monitoring Outlook 1992*, OECD, Paris, and data from *Agricultural Economic Statistics*, Cat. 21-803, Statistics Canada, the "subsidy equivalence" value received by Quebec dairy producers in 1991 was $1.35 billion, out of a total Canadian value received by all milk producers of $2.895 billion.

should stand for this, just as ROC would no doubt apply huge new agricultural tariffs to Quebec-sourced milk.

The United States would no doubt agree. They might then go on to propose to take the same attitude with all supply management arrangements within ROC itself (notwithstanding recent accommodations reached in this area), because *that* deal really wouldn't survive the old Canada either. And why wouldn't they say this? They owe nothing to our protected farming sector, and we would be bargaining from a far weaker position.

In terms of cultural industries, the same logic serves, although Quebec would be in a better position. Quebec possesses the only real available barrier against the might of American culture: language. They don't really need our specially negotiated cultural protections. Why should the Americans continue their special deal for ROC? After all, in law, they may no longer be bound—the party with whom they signed the deal would no longer exist.

This point is worth underlining. ROC must understand that the separation of Quebec will not only open up all of *Quebec's* relationships with the rest of the world, but it may also do the same to ROC in some cases. To repeat, foreigners have entered into deals with *Canada*. Canada at that point will be gone. ROC is not Canada, though it may be a successor.

Parties to any agreements with Canada that for one reason or another would find it convenient to re-open or abrogate such agreements will have some excuse and ability to do so, without even the penalty of international disapproval. (To assist in focusing the attention of Ontario, this could include the Auto Pact, for example.) In other words, what is widely believed in ROC to be a separation penalty for Quebec may also apply to us in some cases—an uninvited penalty perhaps, but a penalty all the same. It should surely not be viewed as a large bargaining threat we have to hold over Quebec, if we feel so inclined, for it cuts vigorously both ways.

These few examples should serve to make the fundamental point: the rest of the world, and especially the Americans, will grieve in principle, and then rapidly and aggressively follow its own interests in practice. The world is a tough place.

Quebec attitudes

As to the other external force, what about the attitude of Quebec, post-referendum? (Assuming the separatists have won.)

To some extent, this will depend upon how the referendum process unfolds and whether the tactics of ROC are seen to be appropriate, or somehow offensive in the circumstances. But no matter *how* offensive ROC may have been (short of actual invasion), there will be a strong tendency to forgive and forget, as far as Quebec is concerned.

After all, they will have "won," in their terms, and winners can afford to be generous. Moreover, they will need ROC, not in any absolute, "we're-dead-otherwise" sense, but because a cooperative ROC will make the world a lot easier for an independent Quebec. Every Quebecker senses this. That is why the Parti Québécois is so insistent on their forecast that ROC will be sensible, rational, and cooperative, no matter what we say now.

That is also why important voices in ROC will argue that we should be just the opposite—that we should not only telegraph our determination to be an implacable enemy of a breakaway Quebec, but we should give hostages to fortune and make irrevocable commitments that will not allow us to be cooperative after separation, even if that *is* the sensible thing to do.

This is a fundamental question of ROC strategy, to be analyzed below. For now, what is important is that the new Quebec can be expected in almost all circumstances to be reasonable and cooperative, not just to ROC, but to anglophones and allophones within Quebec, to international agencies, to foreign capital—in a word, to every force that might help or harm it. This approach is to its advantage, and that will drive and temper its stands on every issue, save such non-negotiable fundamentals as integrity of language, culture, and territory.

The emotions of ROC

And the appropriate attitude for ROC? It really depends on what you want out of the process, it depends on whose interests you are serving, and it depends on your attitude towards risk.

On the first topic—what each of us wants out of the process—we should each have our personal catharsis and get the reactive emotions out of our systems. Many of us will become exceedingly angry, as we contemplate the real possibility of the end of Canada. Some will be angry, because they fought World War II to preserve many things, of which Canada may have been one. (Memory plays tricks. Most were actually fighting for Britain, the Empire, freedom, a job at the end of the Depression, or "our way of life." Canada as a nation was a smaller part of "our way of life" in those days. Our flag was still the Red Ensign, and we sang "The Maple Leaf Forever" in school, a song of the British Empire on which the sun then never set. Indeed, had either World War been *more* about Canada specifically, Quebec would certainly have been a more enthusiastic participant.)

Some will be angry because they just hate change. Some will be angry because they don't like Quebec and that French bunch that Ottawa gives in to all the time, and "they" will finally have won. Some will be angry because their kids have a lot of time invested in immersion school—for what, now? Some will be angry at our governments or political parties, and for good reason.

And some will be angry because they will correctly sense the very direct change this is going to make to our lives—to our mortgage rates, our trading patterns, our standard of living, what we hear on our newscasts, presenting a whole new set of preoccupations in a world that is already quite complicated enough.

There is no getting around such emotions. One can only get *through* them. The best argument for doing so, and doing so as quickly as possible, is of self interest. Angry people make lousy negotiators, and they are easy to manipulate.

Others will not be angry—they will only be sad. A few will say they are pleased; a few will say they don't care. There are many ways of dealing with major events in our lives, and this event will certainly qualify, abstract and far off as it may seem today. We shall all just have to cope, there being no sensible alternative.

Once we get past ourselves and our own emotions, it will be time to think about whose interests we want to serve. Certainly we will want to serve our own interests, and those of our families and friends. And that is about as far as any of us are accustomed to thinking is our civic duty, because that is all that is normally required. The breakup of Canada requires something more.

The grandchildren won't be at the bargaining table

As we go through the days and months of negotiation with Quebec and discussions about the joint or several futures of ROC, the really interested parties won't be at the table at all. Our grandchildren, and theirs, will be the heirs to whatever we do in these circumstances. Thankfully, such upheavals come very seldom. The constitutional patterns we set within a year or two of referendum day will quite possibly endure for generations, and the attitudes we bring to the table will set the climates that will endure for many years at the very least.

In other words, in my opinion, we should try to consider whether the decisions we make in the breakup and reconstituting of Canada and ROC will serve our descendants who—and underline this—will bring no historical baggage of the sort we bear today, *if they are lucky*.

Yes, we can load them down with baggage. We can send Irish-question type messages down over the years, if we really dislike our kids. We can tell our own successors, that, "by God, we were right! And they were wrong!" And, unsaid will be, "the injury never ends, and you kids are going to pay for it."

This would not be unusual—it would even be ordinary, as we see some quarrels of days past being refought around the world today. And in our own land it is a marvel, for example, that we see only some of this in aboriginal Canadians, and not a whole lot more. They have far worse grievances over a century and longer than ROC will ever have against Quebec. But the course of wisdom is always to look to the future, and in particular, for the grandchildren.

All of this argues for calm, for serenity, and for rational deliberation, at a time when many will be screaming for the political equivalent of blood.

There is one more matter to consider, and that is the element of risk. Caution is not a virtue in and of itself. Indeed, if it binds one to the dry decks of the Titanic rather than to those wave-tossed lifeboats so far below, it is foolish. But equally, adventurism in politics can often be deadly, and it is almost always immoral, for leaders place bets with the lives of others in ways that they have not been asked to.

As always, it is the times, the context, that make the rules. Churchill was right to take the risk of war rather than the sure peace (for a time) he could have made with Hitler. But such great and proper risks are rare, and generally in reaction to a greater evil. We shall see no cause for great risks by ROC in reaction to the separation of Quebec. On the contrary, we shall have every cause for prudence.

It is against the law, and you can't do it!

There is and will be a school of thought which says something like the following:

1. What Quebec is doing is wrong, unlawful, injurious to the interests of the rest of us, and we don't have to stand for it.

2. There is a price that Quebeckers will not be willing to pay, if the rest of us are prepared to raise the stakes to that level.

3. This price includes warfare by gradations of economic, political, diplomatic, and eventually military means, as required. (Some will think that "military" goes too far, but if Vietnam proved anything, it is that you are most unwise to commence a fight that you are not prepared to finish.)

4. In the furtherance of the above, it is necessary to teach Canadians outside of Quebec that this is the right thing to do. This involves generating more than a little hatred of Quebec.

5. We plan to win. But if we lose, we will not give up, and the post-facto justification and scorched earth policies will continue. There should be no misunderstanding on that.

Now, put so baldly, this does not make a lot of sense. But there will be those who try to obtain the same effect with less pointed words. And that leads us to the most explosive issue in the entire debate.

Abandonment

"We are Canadians! We do not want to go with the rest of an independent Quebec. You have responsibilities; you must come to our aid!" We will hear this in principle very often as the debate unfolds, and it will become even tougher if identifiable groups in Quebec produce valid evidence of their democratic wish to "stay with Canada" as the rest of Quebec takes its leave.

Sometimes intertwined with the urge to punish, and sometimes distinct from it, is the concern about *abandonment* of moral responsibilities or trusts located within the present boundaries of Quebec. The three areas most commonly cited are those of responsibility to the approximately 57,000 Quebeckers of official native origin,[33] for whom there is a special federal responsibility, the responsibility to the large (about 700,000)[34] population of anglophones in the province, and the responsibility to the Maritime provinces to maintain a land bridge for access. We leave the latter to the "Bargaining with Quebec" chapter, but the first two touch the central core, and determination, of the "attitude" question.

And "determination" is the key. What are the necessary numbers or characteristics of a community in order that it may exercise self-determination? And on a geographical basis, is it a whole province? Riding by riding? Ancient Quebec versus the "new" (turn of the century) Quebec territory, or even poll by poll, as advocated in the Partition solution of Scott Reid, described in Chapter 2?

One thing is certain: an insistence on anything but the existing boundaries of Quebec, except by agreement, will lead to a major con-

---

33 *Census 1991* includes about 50,000 status North American Indian and 6,800 Inuit. There are an additional 8,700 non-status Metis.

34 This is a flexible number. The 1991 census listed 654,000 Quebec residents whose mother tongue is English. There were 568,000 "other," or allophones, and 5,662,000 people with French as their mother tongue. The "home language" numbers were 716,000, 362,000, and 5,604,000 respectively, with some additional "multiple" responses. Finally, a study done for the Conseil de la Langue Francaise found only about one-quarter of Montreal allophones work always or mostly in English.

frontation with the vast majority of the people of that province, whether separatist or federalist. The feeling about the integrity of Quebec's boundaries is absolutely overwhelming. The logic of this is difficult. How do you argue that Quebec can separate from Canada, but that a significant chunk of the north largely populated by natives cannot separate from Quebec? The separatists have no difficulty with this; many others do.

We shall hear a very great deal about this debate as various voices rise over the months to come. In terms of practical politics, two things should be said. One is about emotions; the other is about the deal that may well be reached with native groups. The first matter is that emotion is important—on both sides. For Quebeckers, it is a go-to-the-wall issue, literally. It is the main foreseeable trigger for violence; even civil war. "So what!" say some. Well, first let us think.

In analyzing this question, consider what is involved *vis-à-vis* the identified groups. The concerns centre around continuity of *property rights*, *legal rights* and the regime of law, and *government services*. We must ask ourselves, how would these things be changed if Quebec were to become independent?

The first point to note is obvious: a change in government (which is what we are really talking about here—a different government or "public utility" to provide services) does not change either the land or the buildings or any other physical fact. So what we should be concerned about are *rights*.

Put another way, if it comes to this, one of the non-negotiable bottom lines in dealing with the new Quebec for the negotiators for the old Canada, or ROC, or however it is characterized at that time, must be a proper concern for the rights of minority groups insofar as they have been guaranteed by the former Canada. This is a statement of principle, and if this principle is truly achieved, rights to land, property, and protection of the law will be continued unchanged, *except as to the identity of the administering government*. We return to that point below.

That will be the negotiating duty of the old Canada, and it must spend as much of its bargaining power on these ends as required. Some fear that the old Canada might not have enough clout to do this, but our cooperation will be required in many ways. But more importantly, we will be dealing with civilized and democratic people in the province of Quebec, even if we have a serious difference about the continuity of Canada. What that means is that civilized and democratic guarantees should not be difficult to obtain. Our anger at change should not blind us to this.

Moreover, one should not forget that the native and anglophone minorities are not themselves without very significant bargaining clout to assist this end. Put simply, both parties have an enormous capacity to cause grief to the new Quebec if they are not fairly treated.

The native powers in this regard—beyond their political influence over the negotiators for the old Canada—include the creation of great difficulties in world forums for the new country of Quebec, at a time when it will need the most welcoming attitude it can find. This is important.

The native powers include, as well, the ability to cause great economic disruption, especially in northern Quebec and along the United States border. The ways and means include blockades and even much nastier activity. The resolution of such confrontations could no doubt be handled by the Sûreté Quebec (provincial police), but at a huge cost within Quebec society, and potentially with the old Canada.

And so we come to the second of the two practical points mentioned above, which is this: there is a high probability that the new Quebec will offer native residents a better deal, in terms of self-government, money, and resource revenues and shared management, than would be available by staying in Canada. One need not rely on any concept of generosity for this; it is simply in the best interests of Quebec. The cost is not as high for Quebec as it would be for Canada to offer the same things (Canada has no resources in Quebec to share, and has to worry about setting a precedent all across the country), and Quebec has much motivation to get it done.

The powers of a mistreated anglophone community would likely be exercised in a much simpler, but equally deadly way. They would simply leave, in large numbers. Those who would leave would, of course, be the most mobile, meaning the wealthiest, the healthiest, the youngest, the most employable—in a word, the very people the new Quebec must retain. The old, the welfare receiving, and the unskilled anglophones would likely have to remain, at great ongoing cost to Quebec. This does not make sense to Quebec.

It takes but a moment's thought to realize that this power guarantees the most solicitous treatment of anglophones. The new Quebec will *need* them, and badly. Indeed, it is virtually certain that the constitutional principles and governmental policies of a new Quebec would treat anglophones *better* than is the case today.[35] The rationale for this would be that once Quebec becomes independent, the rules concerning language of education, commercial signs, et cetera could be relaxed, for Quebec would totally control its own destiny at this point.

Honouring guarantees

Now what of the caveat registered above, that all of these negotiated rights are subject to the fair and adequate provision of government services to minorities? How can we be sure that this will happen? How can we be sure that commitments will be honoured? There are two divisions to this thought.

First, as to the technical adequacy of governmental services—how well programs are designed and delivered, soundness of economic planning, management of finances, and so on—well, it would be a brave ROC negotiator to claim that Ottawa's track record (or that of most provinces for that matter) would provide a better service for the citizenry in terms of efficiency. None of our governments have a great deal to brag about. A new Quebec might do a bit better; it might do a bit worse. The general competency of government is not a determining issue.

---

35 This is the author's opinion. There is another school of thought that strongly differs, and says that having walked through fire to achieve independence, and therefore being provably unconcerned about economic consequences, the imposition of the French language on anglophones and allophones would be increased to deliver a sort of non-violent "linguistic cleansing." I record this view chiefly to disagree. One may accept economic pain to achieve objectives, but still have a sensible appreciation of cost-benefit ratios. Losing anglophones who could be retained by a fair language policy would be far too costly in the circumstances.

As to whether the government of Quebec would in fact honour the commitments made to minorities, there is a range of sanctions available if they do not. The simplest, of course, is a graduated response in terms of restricting established trade patterns with ROC, interfering with Seaway traffic bound for Quebec, and so on.[36] If required, these would probably have the required effect. And if not?

That hypothetical question causes some—usually an angry few—to say that this reliance on guarantees to minorities is not good enough. We must "save" those people who do not want to go with Quebec, and to whom we have a responsibility, by removing them and their associated land from Quebec. And we must be prepared to use force if necessary.

At this point we must become very frank, and think what is even more unthinkable than separation. There are some people in ROC—I believe not many, but only time will tell—who argue that in the independence process, a time may come to use military force against even a demonstrably free and democratic Quebec. This view is so dangerous, so subversive of civil dialogue and rational solutions, that it must be discussed, worked out, and—in my opinion—resolutely rejected. (To be technically complete, this position of rejecting force assumes that there will not be any evidence, now or later, of atrocities and human rights abuses that might justify such intervention, based on the necessary United Nations tests. I never expect to see anything remotely resembling this come out of the province of Quebec.)

The issue of force

The ultimate remedy of military threat (and action, if required) that some advocate be undertaken *before* separation makes absolutely no sense at that time. The option would be equally available afterwards if commitments were ignored, and one should never talk of using force

---

36   It is appreciated that such sanctions in support of minorities might contravene the GATT. In the circumstances, I do not worry about the international repercussions. And if GATT wished to authorize Quebec to sanction ROC in return, so be it!

earlier than the optimum time. (It is true that in some military situations the pre-emptive strike is the right way to go. This is not remotely such a case. We are talking about friends and countrymen. They may cease to be the latter, but I hope that they will always be friends.)

There is too much thoughtless talk in ROC of shearing Quebec of its territory, too many statements like: "They can leave—with a postage stamp of land!" This is foolish, unless one is prepared to fight to make good that threat. Unenforced threats simply weaken the perpetrator.

When one presses persons with such views, two responses emerge, in roughly equal proportion in my soundings. Some people say, "Well—I guess what I mean is everything short of force." The views of Quebeckers in respect of boundaries are so strong that this is tantamount to abandoning the argument. This is the foolish unenforced threat.

Others say, "O.K.—if you push us that far, we should use the Canadian military to change the boundaries of Quebec prior to independence in certain circumstances." (The "circumstances" almost always relate to one of the three concerns that opened this section.)

Everyone has a right to their view, but I urge a great deal of caution on this one. Under this scenario, consider what is being said in effect. It is this: "We are so convinced that swapping one type of government (Canada/Quebec) for a new type of government (Quebec only) will be so horrible for some people that we are prepared to go to war, with all of the human, economic, and historic consequences for our children that entails."

Maybe some still say this is the right idea, arguing, for example, that the conflict would be so short and sharp that the consequences would be worth the losses. But what if the so-called advantageous consequences were only that the territory concerned were lucky enough to continue being administered by Ottawa, gaining the implacable hatred of its residual Quebec neighbour, and enjoying no better a life than if Quebec City were running things. Would this make sense?

Proponents of military solutions might want to consider the following line of thought. If we can make a deal with Quebec that does protect minorities and *then Quebec reneges*—maybe that is the very earliest time to consider the military option, and then only under United Nations rules. In my opinion, this is an extremely serious question that should neither be glossed over nor considered lightly.

This issue of abandonment has the potential to completely destroy rational talks between the parties, and even to escalate to unnecessary violence. It is soluble through the negotiation of minority safeguards. We will return to the issue in our "Bargaining with Quebec" chapter. But because of its potentially poisonous nature, it is really a proper part of the question of attitudes.

And in the end, it is only the government which deploys military force, and we trust it to be judicious in that regard. But we do not need a climate of public opinion that pushes it in bellicose directions, or encourages informal terrorist-type activity, short of official action. For all of us, and for our children, we need a resolute climate of non-violence, and the most thorough rebuttal of all those who propose violence.

Constructive futurism

Even if it is sensible not to fight, is it not asking too much for ROC to be cooperative with a separated Quebec? This may indeed be the case for many people within ROC. For example, this is probably asking too much of members of the federal government of the day, who will be terribly emotionally tied up in the whole issue. Not for them the Lincolnesque release of a war of unification in the pursuit of a higher ideal like the end of slavery. (That was not Lincoln's impetus of course, though it did not hurt. The simple preservation of the Union was his goal.)

Rather, these failed federalists will be crushed. That the fault will not have been theirs will be almost irrelevant in their own minds—the disaster occurred on their watch. In this, they will be unfair to themselves, but they will be as human as any of us would be in their places. So indeed, we shall probably want new leaders who will not have been part of the problem, better placed to heal on the one hand, and deal on the other. They will be found.

When all is said and done, it is well to remember the sentiment attributed to the historian Arnold Toynbee: "A national state is not a God. It is a public utility, like a gas works."

The comparison is perhaps deliberately mundane and brutal, but there is a deep truth here. A national state *is* a public utility, and only that.

As a public utility, it is not worth dying for, or even suffering very much for, if we can find a better way. Only basic matters like freedom and food and peace and quiet enjoyment of life for our children are worthy of such sacrifices. If our new arrangements secure such basics as well as did the old—or better—we shall have no cause for complaint.

But putting words on paper is easy. Living an attitude of constructive futurism rather than one of embittered reaction will be a test far more difficult and important than that of facing all the many strategic and technical questions we shall be forced to address. For that reason, something as hard to capture as attitude will be absolutely central to our success.

Chapter 6:
The Doughnut and
Other Shapes

THE GENERAL PRESUMPTION IS THAT after the departure of Quebec, the new Canada will look like a doughnut—surrounding the hole where Quebec used to be. Indeed, there is almost no discussion of any other possibility except among ordinary folk, who as usual talk without embarrassment about things that are politically incorrect.

In the Atlantic provinces, people talk about what will happen if the money from Canada stops coming. They wonder if they will have to join the United States—or if they will be allowed to.

In Newfoundland, being the most recent member of Confederation with memories of a time before Canada, one can hear additional musings—now more wistful than anything after so long—about being independent again.

The heartland of Ontario, of course, hears no such talk. It is difficult to think of being in any way separate from Canada when deep inside you, you know that you *are* Canada. Others may leave, but the Ontario essence will always remain. Some francophones in eastern Ontario and some alienated "westerners" in north-western Ontario may long for freedom from Queen's Park, or at least for counterbalances to it. They know full well that this is not in the cards, and will pass quickly to other subjects.

Saskatchewan and Manitoba are in a very difficult position. They are in the centre of Canada, but are also a long way from anything. They are surrounded by nothing to the north, and by little more than nothing in the empty Great Plains of the United States to the south. In their own way, they have found the best of lives that their geography can provide, safe in the arms of Canada. They have less than 7 percent of Canadian GDP. They do not have the population nor infrastructure necessary for a self-contained economy, and their principal resource exports have been declining in price for years. Still, through a combination of inbound transfer payments for social programs and agriculture and a gradually outbound population seeking jobs or retirement, their people have done reasonably well.

If suddenly placed in a position of lacking an attachment to a money-spigot and beneficent outmigration receiver, they would be in tough shape, enduring a lower standard of living and much higher unemployment. As well, extremely unwise borrowing policies of the last Conservative government of Saskatchewan have left that province in very difficult financial circumstances. Even today it has to clear its budgets with the few New York lenders who will buy their bonds. Without transfer payments, it would be in a financial catastrophe. Both provincial governments are keenly aware of this.

Alberta is in a quite different position. Its government is financially healthy and conservative, and popular in that approach. Its economy is buoyant, despite the long-term erosion in oil prices. The oil industry has made the necessary cost adjustments. The natural gas sector is booming, and looks to do so for the foreseeable future. And Alberta's agriculture is far more diversified. When this is added to a population base 25 percent higher than Saskatchewan/Manitoba combined and a GDP 50 percent higher, you can see that Alberta is in good shape. Indeed, it only needs one thing for actual national state viability: guaranteed transportation links (rail, road, and pipeline) for its products to the outside world.

British Columbia is in an even stronger position than is Alberta. With about 12 percent of Canada's population and a bit more than that in GDP, a more diversified economy, geographical membership in the "Cascadia" concept (from Oregon north through to Alaska), direct access to tidewater, and a growing magnet for Asian investment, B.C. really does have it all. Combined with the politics of the situation, British Columbia—in staying with ROC or going on its own—may become the arbiter of the future shape of Canada if it chooses, for reasons to be elaborated below. And if that is the case, don't bet on the doughnut!

The new British Columbia

This, however, is not yet the conventional wisdom. It is just not *done* to publicly speculate that B.C. might end up as a country on its own, and be rather well off in so doing. Perhaps this is a hangover from the days when "separatist" was a genuine epithet in the mouths of all ROC residents, B.C. included. But something has happened.

The Charlottetown Accord experience was certainly an important part of this change. In that exercise, B.C. provided intellectual leadership on the "No" side for all of Canada. Mel Smith, the retired constitutional adviser to a generation of B.C. governments, was one of the first to speak out in a series of telling articles against the Accord very early on. Then B.C. Liberal Leader Gordon Wilson came out as a "No," and led his provincial party on that side, later joined by Sharon Carstairs of Manitoba. When Preston Manning came on board for the national Reform Party, "No" was already respectable in the West, in spite of the overwhelming array of establishment figures on the other side.

No one was more influential in this regard than the talk show host, Rafe Mair. As a lawyer and former B.C. cabinet minister in charge of inter-governmental affairs under Bill Bennett (whose administration produced some of the most innovative constitutional thinking in the country in the early '80s) Mair was well-equipped to ventilate this topic. In addition, his audience on any given day comprises approximately 10 percent of B.C. voters. This issue quickly came to dominate even ordinary discourse in the province.

As matters unfolded, Quebec was reassured in its dislike of the Accord, and it was clearly not going to be alone, since B.C. felt even more strongly against it. The feeling spread to other parts of the country, and the Accord was history. But the experience left a legacy in British Columbia.

Mair expressed this feeling recently on the air. Talking to a federal minister, he said, "B.C. has a confidence it has never had before. We feel we've been badly used by the federation. And if Quebec goes, we do too." This is just one man's opinion, but it is being said more and more. And if this *is* to be the B.C. attitude, the implications are huge, for B.C. can afford to have that attitude.

This B.C. confidence, of course, is more than political. The dramatic growth in the economy, and the daily vote of confidence from hard working and/or wealthy Asian immigrants is transforming the province. Fully 37 percent of "recent immigrants," those who have arrived since 1981, come from Asia and the Middle East. (In the 1991 census, B.C.'s demographic makeup included 723,000 immigrants, or about 22 percent of the population.) Many newcomers to B.C. care little about the historic English-French or Quebec concerns of the rest of Canada, as long as there is stability in B.C., and that is just a fact of life. This new B.C. perspective has not yet penetrated east of the Rockies, but it may be critical to Canada's future.

In the meantime, analysts across the country who are prepared to discuss a post-Quebec world talk only of the doughnut profile. Indeed, even that is so tentative. It seems necessary to be painfully verbose about how they are not really implying that Quebec will go, that it would be terrible if they did, and under no circumstances is this to be construed as a good thing, et cetera—to the point where total constipation of thought sets in, and we are reduced to rearranging the deck chairs on the ROC, without consideration of potential fragmentation.

But remember the glue—mostly inertia. Since this fact—or not—is so important to our future, let us reconsider the glue. After all, it is fair to say that we in ROC could not even have had this conversation as little as, perhaps, five years ago. It would have seemed too unreal. There was something more to our connection as recently as that. The disintegration of the other sorts of glue has been breath-takingly rapid. Above all, we have lost trust in our federal government, in important parts of the country. (This is not true everywhere, but it is truest in the West, the place that may make the difference.)

The new West

There is a long history of western alienation in Canada, but this has very rarely taken on a separatist flavour. Indeed, it is not by accident that the slogan of the Reform Party at its founding some seven years ago was "The West wants in!" Of course this was partly intended to counter the reasonable fear that the old-line parties would attack Reform as separatist. But also, as Henry Kissinger occasionally used to say of diplomatic statements, it had the additional advantage of being true.

The character of this alienation changed over the course of the Meech Lake-Charlottetown experience, which seared the soul of the nation. The freezeout of the real interests of the West during this process become so clear that you could almost hear the closing of previously open minds. Isolated incidents, like the CF-18 contract (stolen from Winnipeg in favour of Montreal) or the Polar 8 icebreaker (promised to B.C. and cancelled), came to have almost the same symbolic force across the West that the National Energy Policy had a few years earlier when it more or less permanently offended Alberta.

The character today is one of distrust of the system. We went from "The West wants in," through the Triple-E Senate experience, which could be sloganized as "The West demands change," to the feeling of today (at least in B.C. and Alberta), which is, "We don't and won't trust you."

The new attitude in western Canada is almost entirely the creation of the federal government, above all that of the Mulroney years. This is not the place to dwell on that story, but history will show how the vanity and dice-rolling of one prime minister, following on the confrontational legacy of his predecessor, dissolved our national glue. And so we arrive at a time when ROC will have to look in a mirror.

The new ROC

Roger Gibbons of the University of Calgary, in an article entitled "Speculations on a Canada Without Quebec,"[37] has all of the fundamentals

---

37   Kenneth McRoberts and Patrick Monahan (eds.), *The Charlottetown Accord, the Referendum, and the Future of Canada*, University of Toronto Press, 1993, pp. 264-273.

right. On the likelihood of ROC being stable when Ontario makes up 50 percent of the population, he notes that,

> A stable federal system of government is improbable when one of the constituent states or provinces contains 50 per cent or more of the national population. If, as would be the case in Canada, that state or province is also the economic heartland, the media hub, the home of the largest metropolitan centre, the site of the national capital, and the home of the Blue Jays, then a stable federal system is even more unlikely.

But he ignores the possibilities of a ROC other than that of the doughnut since, at the beginning of his analysis, he constrains his thinking to "a state that I assume would encompass the nine remaining provinces and the northern territories." Nevertheless, his insights into the doughnut are extremely valuable and instructive. He says among other things: "Canadians would face much more fundamental institutional reform than was proposed in the Charlottetown Accord." This might include:

- a very strict interpretation of representation by population (disadvantaging the Atlantic and Saskatchewan/Manitoba)
- a congressional form of government (including fixed terms) that would weaken party discipline in return for more effective regional representation
- a reformed Senate to give expression to "territorial, and more important, non-territorial identities including those based on gender and ethnicity," and
- an elected president or prime minister to help knit the country together

He thinks the new system would probably be more centralized.

On the other hand, and in proper recognition of the difficulty in predicting chaos, he leaves open the possibility to the contrary that, "as the federal government implodes the provincial governments may move in on the federal carcass. They, after all, would be the only functioning governments left in the short term."

He suggests, given the huge imbalances of populations, that survival might depend on somehow changing the political debate to issues and institutions that cut across territorial lines, though how this would be done is not clear. But surely, in any case, "the political culture that would be likely to emerge in the more homogeneous Canadian state" would offer less support for minority language rights, official multiculturalism, and aboriginal peoples, due to a new focus in ROC on individualism, in opposition to the kinds of collective rights that have been notionally validated by the Quebec fact.

And on the last (aboriginal) subject, he correctly notes that relatively large and powerful immigrant groups (see above with respect to the B.C. numbers), themselves lacking any sort of constitutional collective protection in a new ROC, would have little patience for special treatment of natives, nor for any historical guilt motivating such treatment. The history of most immigrants, after all, is no bed of roses.

All of this analysis is broadly consistent with our earlier outline in Chapter 4. The trouble is, will everyone in ROC want to live in that kind of a new Canada? Or will the doughnut be eaten instead?

The problem of Ottawa

Part of the answer to this question has to do with the usefulness of the doughnut capital. With this political overview in mind, let us now step back for a moment. To import a concept from the physical sciences, let us try a "thought experiment," in the delightful phrase of Albert Einstein. The experimental question: "What would Canada look like without Ottawa?"

Casting about for analogies for doing without, one thinks of a saying of the feminist movement: "A woman without a man is like a fish without a bicycle." But that seems a bit harsh even for something as unloved as Ottawa. Perhaps if we reach back into our collective childhood experience, it would be more apt to say that Canada without Ottawa would be like Oz without the Wizard.

Readers will recall that on their odyssey to the Emerald City, Dorothy and her friends talked of little else but the Wizard, who, they thought, could solve their problems. While the real movers and shakers in the land of Oz—the good and the wicked witches, the industrious Munchkins, and others—influenced the lives of Dorothy and her friends, they kept their faith in the capital city. And when they got there, the Wizard turned out to be just smoke and mirrors.

Canada is somewhat similar. Our media focus on doings in Ottawa, but the events that affect real people happen mostly in provincial and civic governments. The United Nations and events involving Canadians in the corners of the world take the top of the news, but take the bottom of our interests. Amendments to the Criminal Code have little to do with most of us, and with the few exceptions listed below, the rest of Ottawa comprises just incredibly expensive and complicated machinery for churning around money and incurring debt.

The things that Ottawa does fall into two categories: those things that already are, or should be, done by provinces, and those things that really are nation-state in their nature. Here is a list.

Nation-state duties:

- Foreign Affairs and Defence
- Citizenship
- Immigration
- Federal debt servicing
- Currency
- Customs

Current federal duties which overlap with existing provincial duties or "could be" provincial:

- Fisheries
- Employment and Training
- UIC
- Environment
- Agriculture
- Statistics
- Coast Guard
- Pensions
- Criminal law
- Prisons
- Police
- Maps and Surveys
- Forestry
- Tourism
- Housing

- Native Affairs
- Labour

The list is not intended to be exhaustive, but it is illustrative. Intrinsically messy or argumentative items, like labelling, communications, food and drugs, and so on, have not been included, nor have been commercial activities like airlines, railroads, oil companies, and postal delivery which could be done by anyone.

The point for the purpose of this exercise is to illustrate that if Ottawa were to vanish overnight, the duties on the second list could be absorbed by all the provinces without any conceptual difficulty, and probably with some considerable increase in efficiency and responsiveness to local conditions. Practical matters like the movement of personnel to new locations and the redistribution of tax revenue would be the only issues of great import.

So if Canada were to break up through the departure of Quebec and subsequent fragmentation, those "provincial" duties would really require no change in government structure, and, as noted, that includes most duties that governments perform. There remain, however, the "nation-state" duties—and they are important—that would somehow have to be looked after.

Economic geography of subdivision

At this point, it is time to look at the basic geographic and economic units of our country. In looking at the components of Canada without Quebec, I have analyzed four "pieces of the ROC" as the smallest probable units of fragmentation: the Atlantic, Ontario, Alberta, and B.C. Further comment is required on three things: the concept itself, the Atlantic as an entity, and also Saskatchewan/Manitoba. This Prairie duo has its own sections in the tables that follow, but it almost certainly will not be a surviving national state.

On the concept of examining sub-units, we simply must deal with the possibility that the doughnut will not hang together. Indeed, from a western perspective, that may be the most likely scenario if Quebec leaves. (The better scenario for everyone, "Plan C," will be very tricky to arrange.)

On the other hand, there is clearly a limit to useful fragmentation. I think, for example, it is most unlikely that any *sub*-provincial unit would emerge. The tradition of provincial boundaries is very strong, and the only functioning governmental units capable of nation-state duties would be those at the provincial level. Thus Ontario, huge though it is, would be unlikely to divide further.[38]

As mentioned previously, the Atlantic *might* divide further, as there are four functioning governments involved. The history of Newfoundland and the island geographical distinctness of P.E.I. give some argument in that direction. As to the latter, however, it is really too small to carry the apparatus of a national state. Newfoundland is just too poor and insufficiently diversified to really contemplate complete independence.

That is not to say that one or more of the Atlantic provinces might not reach a deal with the United States to enter into some sort of dependency or protectorate arrangement (the possibility of Atlantic statehood within the U.S. is discussed later), but a more likely, or at least interim step would seem to be an Atlantic confederation, with the "national" machinery being based perhaps in Charlottetown as this arrangement avoids giving this plum to any of the three larger provinces, and defers the pain of rationalization of governmental services.

Regarding the establishment of Saskatchewan/Manitoba as a nation-state, figures are presented for the region as a stand-alone, even though attainment of that ultimate status is highly unlikely. They will almost certainly form a relationship with either Ontario or Alberta, or a B.C./Alberta grouping. At this stage, however, it is difficult to predict which way the ties would run—to the east, or to the west.

To the west lie the ports through which most of the Saskatchewan/Manitoba agriculture is shipped; there too is the most vital and

---

38   If Ontario *were to* subdivide into three or four new provinces, it would do a great deal to assist in solving one of the largest political problems militating against an ongoing ROC, namely, the overwhelming size of Ontario. This would lead to an important change in the dynamics. However, as we have seen throughout human history, it is extremely rare that an established government apparatus voluntarily dismembers itself.

growing region of the continent. But the B.C./Alberta partners would almost certainly decline to continue the arrangement of subsidies that Saskatchewan/Manitoba has come to rely upon. This would mean very considerable belt-tightening and outmigration.

To the east lies the alternative wheat port, the market for hydrocarbons the two provinces produce, and, perhaps most importantly, a neighbour well accustomed to the subsidy of regions for alleged mutual benefit. The politics and psychology might make for a more comfortable fit, particularly if—as seems likely—Ontario were to have a problem coming to grips with the new political situation. A little bit of the old empire might seem better than none. (While it is a bit of a stretch, and a far more costly one, Ontario might have the same yearning for the Atlantic region.)

At this point, it will be useful to set out some of the hard data available on all of these actual or potential entities. By no means do the physical and economic facts fully govern how any political organism will behave, but they are important. Table 6.1 compares Canada, ROC, and Quebec. Table 6.2 looks at ROC, its components, and some combinations thereof.

It is obvious from these tables that all entities are quite normal in the world ranking as to GDP and population of the two hundred-plus nation states now in existence, even though the debt is serious on a world scale. What is a little more surprising is how well the smaller fragments compare. For example, Atlantic Canada has a GDP higher than those of almost three-quarters of the world's nation-states. Canada West ranks as about the twentieth largest economy worldwide. Even British Columbia alone is about thirty-fifth. On the face of it, these are all viable states. (Note: the northern territories are not included in this particular analysis.)

Of course, some are more viable than others! This is partly due to the differing debt burdens, especially in comparison to ability to service the debt. But part of the reason is hidden, showing up in the next table, which describes certain internal transfers which would presumably disappear along with Canada, or with the subsequent disappearance or non-formation of ROC. (One should not, however, overlook the possibility that richer regions striking out on their own might agree to a sort

Table 6.1: The Doughnut's Statistics Compared

	ROC	Quebec	Canada
Population 1994 (millions)	21.734	7.240	28.974
Rank in the world by population (in 1990)	42	92	32
Land mass (sq. km)	7,858,640	1,540,680	9,970,610
GDP 1994 estimate (millions of $)	570,081	167,549	737,630
Rank in the world by GDP in 1990	8	19	7
Total Net Debt, 1994 estimate (millions of $)[a]	597,087	224,229	821,316
Net Debt per capita, 1994 ($)	27,472	30,971	28,347
Net Debt as a percentage of GDP, 1994	104.7%	133.8%	111.3%
Debt Charges, 1994 estimate (millions of $)	53,173	17,689	70,862
Debt Charges per capita, 1994 ($)	2,447	2,443	2,446
Trade Balance with the Rest of the world, 1989 (millions of $)[b]	3,898	-5,876	-1,978

(The assumption is made that the fragments accept their per capita share of the federal debt.)
[a]The federal net debt and debt charges are allocated regionally according to population. Net debt and debt charges are Fraser Institute estimates.
[b]Only the Balance of Trade in goods and services is available since there are no data on transfers by region.

Source: *The Canadian World Almanac 1993*; *The Daily*, August 24, 1993, Statistics Canada; *Public Sector Assets and Liabilities*, cat. 68-508, Statistics Canada, March 1994; *Canadian Economic Observer*, catalogue 11-010, Statistics Canada; data from the Public Institutions Division of Statistics Canada; *Provincial Outlook*, Spring 1994, Conference Board of Canada, April 14 1994; Federal & Provincial budgets, estimates & public accounts; "Inside Canada's Government Debt Problem and the Way Out," Robin Richardson, *Fraser Forum*, The Fraser Institute, May 1994.

Table 6.2: ROC Divided Six Ways

	R.O.C.	Atlantic Provinces	Ontario	Sask. & Manitoba	Alberta	British Columbia	West
Population 1994 (millions)	21.734	2.391	10.847	2.120	2.681	3.599	8.400
Rank in world by population, 1990	42	136	68	141	134	124	84
Land mass (sq. km)	7,858,640	502,280	891,190	1,119,060	644,390	929,730	2,693,180
GDP 1994 estimate (millions of $)	570,081	45,943	295,553	47,490	78,476	97,237	223,203
Rank in world by GDP in 1990	7	53	14	51	38	35	19
Total Net Debt, 1994 estimate (millions of $)[a]	597,087	68,927	298,675	58,503	68,033	86,916	213,452
Net Debt per capita, 1994 ($)	27,472	28,828	27,535	27,596	25,376	24,150	25,411
Net Debt as a percentage of GDP, 1994	104.7%	150.0%	101.1%	123.2%	86.7%	89.4%	95.6%
Debt Charges, 1994 estimate (millions of $)	53,173	6,193	24,509	6,569	7,238	8,414	22,214
Trade Balance with the rest of the world, 1989 (millions of $)[b]	2,090	-8177	12,741	-2,090	1,742	-1,719	-2,067

[a]The federal net debt and debt charges are allocated regionally according to population. Net debt and debt charges are Fraser Institute estimates.

[b]Only the Balance of Trade in goods and services is available since there are no data on transfers by region. The "rest of the world" includes the provinces which do not form part of the named region.

Source: *The Canadian World Almanac 1993*; *The Daily*, August 24, 1993, Statistics Canada; *Public Sector Assets and Liabilities*, cat. 68-508, Statistics Canada, March 1994; *Canadian Economic Observer*, catalogue 11-010, Statistics Canada; data from the Public Institutions Division of Statistics Canada; *Provincial Outlook*, Spring 1994, Conference Board of Canada, April 14, 1994; Federal & Provincial budgets, estimates & public accounts; "Inside Canada's Government Debt Problem and the Way Out," Robin Richardson, *Fraser Forum*, The Fraser Institute, May 1994.

of transitional "foreign aid" to poorer regions, probably in debt servicing assistance.)

Federal transfers to provinces

The figures in table 6.3 must be handled with some degree of caution. For example, the provincial allocation of such federal expenditures as defence or foreign affairs can only be made on the basis of some fairly arbitrary assumptions. Other federal transfers such as payments to persons can be more precisely accounted for, but procurement is difficult to deal with, as is the true province of origin of much tax revenue. But with the necessary caveats, these tables can be useful for our purposes. And one should keep in mind that the debt and deficit numbers have deteriorated markedly since the latest available year for this series, which is fiscal 1990/91, or three full years ago. Also in table 6.3, it is worth paying particular attention to the last two columns, which charge each region with the population ratio share of the federal deficit

Table 6.3: Federal Government Spending Net of Interest and Taxes by Province, 1990/91

	Federal Spending net of Interest	Federal Taxes	Net Inflow	Share of Federal Deficit	Net Inflow less Federal Deficit
	(millions of $)				
Atlantic Provinces	15,857	7,430	8,427	2,800	5,627
Quebec	27,495	24,473	3,022	8,184	-5,142
Ontario	34,587	53,328	-18,741	11,761	-30,502
Saskatchewan & Manitoba	10,084	7,569	2,515	2,516	-1
Alberta	9,100	11,282	-2,182	2,983	-5,165
British Columbia	11,446	15,324	-3,878	3,779	-7,657

Source: Isabella Horry and Michael Walker, *Government Spending Facts 2*, The Fraser Institute, 1994.

that will have to be looked after by that region. Since Ottawa spends about four dollars every year for each three that it collects, it is easy to think that we are all getting something for nothing, unless we account for the rise in our indebtedness. So the table illustrates, for example, that while Saskatchewan/Manitoba looked like $2.5 billion winners on the surface, after this deduction it was near zero. For Quebec, the situation is the opposite. An apparent $3.0 billion "profit" turns into an actual $5.1 billion "loss." The deficit is so huge that we cannot ignore it in these calculations.

The first and most alarming impression is how reliant we have become on continued borrowing to maintain our standard of living. The apparent federal largesse in many parts of the country looks much less attractive when the associated debt increase is factored in. This sort of information leads the poorer regions to wonder how they could possibly cope on their own, and the others to wonder how they could possibly afford to remain associated with such a financial mess. Indeed, as mentioned before, that is one of the arguments of the Quebec separatists, and is illustrated by the above figures. Their claim is that Quebec will be better able to manage its finances once independent, but under the hypothesis of this book, that will no longer be our affair—unless, of course, they can't pay for their share of history.

The second impression shows the dramatic differences between regions, whether they donate or receive cash as a result of our current federal system. The obvious conclusion is that this is unsustainable, whatever Quebec may choose to do. The whole pattern of federal expenditure—not just regional transfers—has only been possible through the profligate use of other people's money, which will become increasingly hard to get, especially if we not only continue to show no signs of mending our ways, but are involved in a unity crisis as well.

This factor may indeed have a good deal to do with the ability of ROC to split up. At the present time, as mentioned in a previous chapter, Canada requires about $25 billion of foreign cash per year to support its current account imbalance and standard of living. Having Quebec in or out won't change that reality by much.[39]

That is a lot of cash. It is only given by lenders who believe they will be paid back. They can barely believe this to be true of Ontario even today. These lenders would not have any degree of comfort at all with an Atlantic or Saskatchewan/Manitoba detached from Canada or ROC. Some say this would mean that the more affluent sections of the country would have to enter into cross-guarantees of the old federal debt on some basis, should they themselves wish to continue to have unimpeded access to international capital markets. That would be a serious constraint.

Others say that foreign lenders would be happy to continue doing business with, say, Alberta as long as the province looked solid, and it continued to do the honourable thing and service its 9.25 percent share (based on population) of the old federal debt, rolling that percentage of maturing debt into new Alberta debt as the federal paper comes due. According to this theory, lenders are now used to taking haircuts on sovereign debt, however much they may hate it, and business with good customers goes on.

The third impression from the above three tables is that of current account viability in terms of receipts and payments to the rest of the world (here meaning other parts of Canada as well). This measure, of course, adds the whole of private sector activity to the government flows, concluding that Ontario and the two western provinces are very solid in this regard, and the others are not. This has currency implications as well, in the sense of making possible a simple adoption of the United States currency by such an entity, if required.

It would be a mistake to make too much of the above numbers, because any community involves a great many more values. Some of

---

39 The only thing that will change that reality, of course, is some combination of a lower standard of living and higher productivity, both of which shifts are already being imposed on Canada by circumstances. The only real question is whether there will be a large, wrenching one-time adjustment which could be triggered by the breakdown of the national state, or a gradual accommodation to the financial facts of life.

the other values are intangible, and some support the voluntary transfer of resources based on theories of common welfare. But, like it or not, realities like the above will have a great deal to do with bargaining positions within ROC after Quebec goes. Moreover, if ROC splits up, or even if only Quebec goes, the new circumstances will induce and/or force major changes in these numbers to accommodate the new realities. In other words, these are starting points that signal economic depth or necessary adjustments.

So based on all the above, what is "Plan B" (which, after all, is the title of this book)? The only thing we can say for sure at this point, is that "Plan B" is not obvious. It will have to be worked out, because it is a political question that will depend on what people want, while they haven't even started to ask the necessary questions on which to base their thinking. But we can be sure that there will be some things that just won't work.

If Plan B is the continuation of ROC, what will the structures and relationships be—for clearly the old ones aren't sustainable, even if Quebec doesn't leave. And if "Plan B" is some kind of fragmentation, what will the units be, what will be the terms of their separation be, and what will their ongoing special relationships be, if any?

In Chapter 8 we will get into viability analysis for the ROC and split-up scenarios, and—perhaps more importantly at this point—we will discuss the machinery we shall need to carry on those discussions in a productive way. That will be the second of our two talks among Canadians. For now, we turn to the first discussion, with Quebec.

Chapter 7: Bargaining with Quebec—Machinery and Issues

D IVORCES ONLY HIT THE NEWSPAPERS in these modern times if they are large enough or strange enough. Vancouver had a case a few years ago involving much money and a lot of anger. While the lawyers argued over dollars and assets, the thick-walleted husband paid a visit to his estranged wife's garage and helped himself to the snow tires for her car. (People from Vancouver do not like the world to know they use snow tires, but it's true.)

Now, the gentleman in question did not need those tires for himself. Somehow he just felt better that the other side didn't have them. The judge didn't think much of that and said so, but such is human nature. And the negotiations between Quebec and ROC (however represented) will be carried on between groups of human beings with complex motives. The problem is how to avoid the snow tire syndrome.

This is important, because we live in a democracy, and people's feelings will inevitably affect the bargaining process with Quebec. The emotions may be higher or lower after the referendum has passed, which is the continuing premise of this book, depending on the emotional climate during the referendum campaign, the narrowness of the result, and the attitude of the "winners."

Thus, even though we will be wise to deliberately insulate the members of the negotiating team from daily political pressures, discussed below, they will not be able to ignore the background music, especially if it should endanger their negotiating mandate. Public opinion will be very important.

Viewed from an emotional point of view, most of ROC will be in a grieving process—grieving for the old ways, the old Canada, the framework and background that has contained our lives if we are born here, or has redefined our lives if we are immigrants. This is no small emotional loss. Indeed, it is enormous. And since different people handle grief with varying degrees of stoicism or excitement, we will see some very dramatic demonstrations of adverse feeling.

The stages of our grief

The classic stages of grief include first denial, then anger, bargaining, and finally acceptance. Of course, some people never get through all of the phases to final acceptance of whatever their own realities may be. This invariably leads to less happiness than would otherwise be the case, but again, this is human nature. Some people will never, ever forgive Quebec and/or Quebeckers for separating. Others will get on with their lives.

Individuals have that choice. National states do not. States, such as ROC or its fragments will be, simply must get on with their lives. They can do it after a terrible waste of life and treasure, as is the case in the former Yugoslavia, or in some more intelligent way. But at the end of the day, as in the diplomatic maxim, states can have no permanent friends or enemies or sentiments—only interests.

At this writing, many people in ROC—perhaps most—are still in the "denial" phase. It is commonly believed that either Quebec will not want to secede, or, if it does, that it will come to see that it cannot afford to do so. By the time of a referendum affirming separation, if that is what happens, these same people should be well into the "anger" stage, unless they have either already passed through it, or have seen other possibilities. This latter state is exactly what we should all try to encourage, because anger is the enemy of sound decisions. Bad decisions will be paid for not just by ourselves, but also by our children, so we really do not have the right to indulge our annoyances.

Good for us, not bad for them

Above all, this means being motivated in our thinking about bargaining with Quebec *strictly on the basis of what is good for us*, and most definitely *not* on the basis of what is bad for them. We can't afford to chase after snow tires, even, as we shall see, in cold and snowy Ungava, in northern Quebec. We need to rationally follow our self-interest, not our emotions.

This point is so fundamentally important that it must be built into the design of our negotiating machinery from the very beginning. But this has to be a conscious choice, for every reader will be aware that this commitment to common sense is exactly what the separatists want. A large part of their message to Quebeckers is that the new country need not fear any irrational acts of vengeance by the rest of Canada. They will obtain their first "win," if you like, if and when ROC decides to be rational in bargaining. This will be a big first bitter pill to swallow for most people.

As is the case in assessing all unpleasant medicine, one must look at the alternative, which in this instance is to adopt a deliberate policy of escalating on a graduated menu of ways to injure Quebec—especially in ways that don't hurt ROC too much. For example, while our spite would not likely persuade us to risk our soldiers in a shooting war, some might support guerilla activity, especially in native and anglophone areas. (The underlying rationale would be to make northern Quebec, for example, so expensive that it would be given quasi-independence.)

We might systematically obstruct Quebec's attempts to accede (or succeed, as they would argue) to membership in international trade and diplomatic organizations of value: the U.N., GATT, NAFTA, et cetera. We might deny the direct use of the Canadian banking settlement system to Quebec and its residents. Though this could be circumvented, it would cause difficulties.

We could close our borders to products of Quebec manufacture or agriculture, which would have definite effects, particularly in the time it takes to replace markets, often at lower prices. We could attempt to impede Quebec-destined navigation in the Gulf of St. Lawrence, forbid the export of parts and machinery from ROC to Quebec, and initiate numerous other nasty activities. The question is, why would one want to do such things?

One can make a case for the use of threats in a bargaining process, though the wisdom of this is very problematic, especially if a failure in the process then requires the threat to be carried out. But there is at least a rational argument to that approach.

On the other hand, it is absolutely impossible to make a rational argument for acts in this circumstance that would be designed simply to *punish*. (This is not always the case in international matters, of course. For example, it was entirely rational to punish Saddam Hussein in the Gulf War, with the objective being to modify future behaviour. That does not apply here.)

One may say the same thing about acts designed to "get even." These may bestow some feelings of satisfaction that individuals can enjoy. Again, for national states, the satisfaction is very transitory, and the results enduring. For example, it might be satisfying to burn down the Chinese Consulate in Toronto or to stop shipping wheat in protest of Tiananmen Square, but then what? Even if we feel good the day after, what about a month or a year or a decade later? As one or more new national states, ROC will have to think in these time frames.

The conclusion one reaches upon thinking about it a bit is rather simple: our better approach will be rational and unemotional, strictly pursuing our own interests in the negotiations, without attempting to punish or get even with Quebec. One would not wish to deny our negotiators the ability to wield an occasional sharp elbow in tight corners to seek our advantage, but in general, our advantage will not come through a beggar-thy-neighbour policy. Indeed, it is quite the contrary. One wants prosperous neighbours, both as good customers and as allies in the great twenty-first century strategic challenge of improving the lot of the developing world.

This does *not* mean that we should not attempt to squeeze every little advantage possible out of the situation at the bargaining table. Quite the contrary—we will have some cards to play in this regard, and the essence of rationality and pursuit of our own advantage is to play them in the most profitable way we can, even if that costs our old friends across the Ottawa River.

Negotiating machinery

All this leads to the first and second principles for whatever negotiating machinery may end up acting for ROC, which are:

1. The public should be fully informed as to the approach of the negotiators, and means should be found, perhaps through provincial legislatures, to endorse that approach.

2. The approach should be one of strict self-interest for ROC. Negative tactics should be used cautiously, and always towards a positive end rather than for a negative purpose.

   In the second principle, it will be noted that the phrase "the self-interest of ROC" begs the possibility that different parts of ROC might have rather different self-interests. This will be dealt with below.

   With a general approach established, it will be necessary to have some preliminary debate within ROC on how to handle specific issues. This has advantages as well as dangers. The danger of such discussion, from a negotiator's point of view, is that it tends to reduce flexibility. The advantage is that only with some minimum level of advance assent can negotiators be reasonably assured of coming up with a package that will "sell" to their principals. This brings us to a third principle.

3. Thus, there should be an advance public discussion of major issues.

   Productive discussion of complex and emotional issues requires good leadership and facilitation. A special responsibility will fall on the "chattering classes," the pundits and editorialists, open-liners and journalists, academics and opinion leaders of all kinds, to carry this discussion.

   A few of them may even be able to help shape the discussion, but this cannot be left to chance. There simply must be political leadership here, and that leads to the fourth principle.

4. ROC must create a steering committee to guide the negotiating process that is broadly representative of its constituency, trusted for this purpose, and capable of clear communications with public and expert interest groups, in both directions.

   It is general experience in protracted and complex negotiations that the actual face-to-face work should be done by skilled practitioners. The negotiators are virtually always afforded some insulation from daily pressures to get their work done. But in most successful tag teams of this sort, they are also closely reporting to and instructed by the sort of steering committee discussed in point 4. The next principle therefore, follows.

5. ROC, through its steering committee, must select a team of negotiators to do the actual dealings, reporting to and buffered by the steering committee.

We are then left with three major questions, which are:

- How do we constitute the Steering Committee?
- What are the major issues that must be discussed with the electors of ROC in advance?
- How should ROC stand on those issues?

Before proceeding in this vein, let us once again note a point that we must never forget if we have to pass through this breaking up process. It is this: important as this Quebec discussion is, it is *not* the major business of ROC at this point in time. These negotiations will essentially be for tidying up the past and, as is all too usual, playing to Quebec's agenda. The truly important work of ROC, to be carried out by other players on other fields, will be to design its own future. The corollary of this, in designing bargaining machinery, is that we must not let the lesser bargaining issue tie our leaders up in knots, when they and we have far more important things to do, relative to our future.

Steering the bargaining process

And how do we constitute the steering committee? Is it the federal government? Or is it something else?

Imagine Canada the day after Quebec has voted to leave in a free and fair referendum! The economic calculus, which will identify a lot of losers, will sink in slowly. The politics of the situation will be immediate. In political terms, there is just one loser at this point, and that loser is the federal government. This is not a little loss. It is an enormous, crushing, worst-in-Canada's-history loss. It really is unthinkable that the loser could continue to govern with any real authority.

Is it fair to say that the federal government would be *the* loser? Well, who else? You can bet that most of the provinces will not have their heads very far out of the trenches on this one. Virtually every premier who initially approved of the Meech Lake deal was wiped out at or before the next election. Most of today's premiers were so burned by the Charlottetown Accord that they now have a healthy respect for the dangers of taking on constitutional files that they can't control.

Moreover, the linguistic and political implications of a referendum battle in Quebec pretty well rule out direct participation by the premiers in any case. They will surely give all support to the federal government—all support short of real political risk for them, that is. They will have sufficient excuses to cover such lack of action, starting with alleged, and perhaps actual, counterproductive effects of intervening in a "family feud," or seeming to exert "anglo" pressure in Quebec. And they will have a genuine excuse as well: there has to be somebody of political leadership with credibility left in the country if a referendum is lost.

So assuming such a loss, what will we be left with in Ottawa? Unless there is an unexpected personnel change between now and a referendum, we will have a government headed by a prime minister from a Quebec constituency, with his two most important lieutenants, the Ministers of Finance and Foreign Affairs, from Quebec as well. The two most powerful provinces of ROC, Ontario and British Columbia, are already loudly on record in complaining about the weakness of their provinces' federal cabinet representation. But the real problem of government credibility is more simply stated. You don't hire losers to go out and fight your battles.

But there is an even greater problem for Ottawa at this point, far beyond that of the actual government. That is the problem of major conflict of interest. The entire federal apparatus will be entrapped in this conflict because the things that will need to be done at this stage will involve many matters which will be terribly injurious to the nuts and bolts of the national capital: the power, the jobs, even the basic real estate values of homes and retirement benefits that so many lives have been built around.

This is especially true in designing what is to become of ROC, for whatever it is will almost certainly gut the employment base of Ottawa, including senior executives. But even in dealing with Quebec, the new relationships can be designed to be more or less complex, requiring more public servants and power in Ottawa, or not. One may be sure that official Ottawa would do its best to rise above such conflicts of interest. One may be equally sure that much of ROC would not want to take that risk.

There are two potential solutions. One involves the provinces; the other involves an election. But note that *neither can be forced* on the government of the day. There is no short-term machinery to force the federal government to do *anything*, as long as it controls Parliament. As Brian Mulroney demonstrated conclusively, a prime minister with terrified backbenchers can control Parliament long past the time when hardly another breathing entity in ROC would support him for dogcatcher.

In other words, paralysis for some period of time is a distinct possibility. This is important for those who have mobility options to more stable countries, whether it be mobility of their persons or of capital. Paralysis by a ticking clock of enormous foreign debt is not affordable. But it could happen.

Provinces to the rescue?

Whenever the paralysis is resolved, let us consider first the option perhaps most palatable to Ottawa as it does not involve honourable resignation, which is a near lost art in Canadian politics. We bring in the provinces. The federal government could plausibly design a First Ministers' Steering Committee to oversee the negotiations with Quebec. It would be fraught with dangers, but it would pass the first "smell" test for legitimacy.

The dangers relate to representativeness and to talents. Were this committee to be representative of ROC for this purpose, it would only be by happy accident. As a major example, the current premiers of Ontario and B.C., the two largest provinces of ROC, may well have still avoided an election prior to the time under consideration. Each government has a lower percentage of support in its respective province as at this writing than the percentage who believe that Elvis Presley is still alive.

And further regarding representativeness, this forum would give P.E.I. the same voice as Ontario. (In ordinary First Ministers' meetings, which are not concerned with such great matters and are checked and balanced by a strong federal presence, this does not much matter. In the circumstances we have under consideration, it does.)

As to talents, the premiers concerned, *and their advisers*, have all been chosen to deal with issues far removed from the important business of the day. This is not said in any disrespect, but the questions for consideration in the separation of Quebec have little to do with the business of running a provincial government, where, the province of Quebec aside, constitutional affairs rank as a nuisance standing somewhere between Greenpeace and mosquitoes.

There is one more thing emanating from the above. This First Ministers group would not have a mandate for their purpose, when one would never be more necessary. Of course, no one at the moment has a mandate to negotiate the division of the country. Their only support, then, would be post-facto their negotiations, i.e., a ROC referendum approving the deal with Quebec. This would be a very dicey call, and the looming presence of such a test would significantly impair the negotiating strength and imagination of this group.

That said, you settle for what you can get in this life, and the above might be it. Great times often truly do call forth greatness in people, and may do here as well.

Or an election?

The option less palatable to the government (though not to "Ottawa" because its lead role as capital of the country is at least briefly maintained) is for the government to resign and call for an election to select the leaders for this new circumstance. Hard cheese indeed! Let us review in point form the features of such a move from the governing party's view:

- lose job—maybe pension
- go down in history as loser—maybe quitter
- perhaps watch that definite non-Liberal Preston Manning take over what is left of things.

But surely these are questions for smaller minds. A broader viewpoint would see that an election move would do the following:

- mandate negotiators for a tough job that truly needs a mandate
- allow for the escape from a really impossible situation (for the losing federal government) with honour intact
- buy precious credibility and time with Quebec, and with the rest of the world.

Time is the friend of ROC, *and* of Quebec, if it can be had at a low cost. It will allow time for thinking and maturity on both sides of the Ottawa River. Both sides will quickly see that the tiger it rides is larger than it thought. Of course, the rest of the world must see this delay as a plus as well, as time to be our friend. That takes us back to what the principal players will have to say on Day 1, to reassure our foreign creditors.

Such an election would be as fascinating to political aficionados as it would be horrifying to old line politicians. This would be a totally focused event—no electoral bribes with our money, no political correctness, no undeliverable nonsense about jobs—just straight, hard reality therapy. The federal political world would be turned upside down! And unlike every election since confederation, there would be zero attempt to purchase support in Quebec, except under one bizarre scenario.[40]

The focus of the election would be twofold—who would be best to negotiate with Quebec, and who would be best to help restructure ROC? One cannot today foresee which task would be seen as more important by the electorate, though in the run of history, it has been the latter, hands down.

Today's bet says Reform would sweep the ROC electorate by default, given the weakness of all of the traditional parties. The Liberals'

---

40 The Liberals and Conservatives, separately or jointly, might try to run "United Canada" candidates in Quebec, promising to refashion confederation if elected. As Quebec has heard this several times before, it would be a tough sell, for reasons based on experience. Under any scenario foreseeable today, the Bloc Québécois would then again run candidates and would win most ridings. But politics is unpredictable, and were this ploy tried in scary international circumstances where Quebeckers had a failure of nerve, who knows?

record would be that of recently having lost the unity of the country, the Tories' status as a two-seat party with a Quebec leader would present problems, to put it mildly, and the NDP has nothing to contribute on this issue. You never know—the Natural Law party could make Official Opposition status yet!

The issues with Quebec

In due course, and however arrived at, a negotiating committee for ROC will be in place. Now it is time to look at the issues. This is well-canvassed ground, and is not the main focus of this book, though it has received most of the attention to date. Speaking as ROC, our settlement with Quebec will be far less important than the settlement among ourselves. What follows, therefore, is but a précis of the main points at issue.[41]

The main questions are these:
- Boundaries
- Currency
- Debt
- Trade

There are subsections within each of the above. We will tackle them in turn.

Boundaries constitute, at once, the most emotional and most straightforward of the topics. The main issue is simply put. Quebec's territory was massively increased by the addition of old Hudson's Bay Company lands, which had previously been deeded to Canada. This was done under Acts of Parliament of 1898 and 1912. The territory in question is generally described as the James Bay region and Ungava. It includes the huge hydroelectric capacity of the James Bay Project, plus extensive mineral resources, and much cold weather.

The demographics are important, as many people in ROC think that these lands should in some way be repossessed. But if you believe in the

---

41 For a more comprehensive survey, especially in economic terms, see *The Economic Consequences of Quebec Sovereignty*, Patrick Grady, The Fraser Institute, 1991.

views of the residents of the area, there may be a problem. As Scott Reid points out, "contrary to myth, northern Quebec is full of French people. The population of the territory transferred to Quebec in 1898 and 1912 is currently over 80 percent French-speaking. The part of the north that traditionally belonged to the Cree today contains more French-Canadians than natives."[42] In other words, Quebec has effectively occupied its north.

The native inhabitants are largely anglophone and have direct links to the federal government, through law, custom, and dollars. The native inhabitants are also skilled practitioners of the bargainer's and publicist's arts, clearly evidenced by a long-running show pitting them against the soap-opera villain of Hydro-Quebec.

To frame the question of the future simply, the natives could say that if Quebec is leaving Canada, then they want to leave Quebec, in a full or partial sense. They will want control over the territory, as well as guaranteed access to funding. They could call upon obligations of the British Crown, and much reference could be made to environmental destruction, Robert Kennedy Jr. and other American friends, and apprehended genocide. We would all do the same thing to enhance bargaining clout in what is, after all, an extremely serious challenge to an imperfect, but known, status quo.

They could say that if self-determination applies to Quebec, it necessarily applies to *parts* of Quebec, and further, "that is what we want, and we call upon the decency and morality and basic humanity of ROC to back us up." This will strike enormous chords of solidarity with many people.

Most Quebeckers will have a rather different point of view. They will suggest that boundaries of emerging states under international law are exactly as they were at the time of separation. They will remind us that, under our constitution, Quebec's boundaries (or those of any province) can only be changed by assent of the province, so the new boundaries will clearly be exactly the same as the old.

---

42   *Canada Remapped*, Arsenal Pulp Press, Vancouver, 1992.

They will state, with reason, that Quebec has signed by far the most comprehensive agreements with aboriginals in Canadian history in the James Bay accords, and that in those agreements the Cree and Inuit have explicitly and unambiguously renounced all of their land claims. They will say that no natives in Canada have been treated more fairly, that they (Quebeckers) are in possession, that they plan to remain so, and that is that.

The northern Quebec boundaries issue is, in other words, totally political, in the finest and most difficult sense of the word.

It is also potentially military, to use a more explosive word. The hugely capital-intensive installations that make James Bay-Ungava so valuable to Quebec, the dams and transmission lines, are extremely vulnerable to sabotage. They are indeed virtually indefensible, except by a total police state. Granted that we are dealing with a low-conceal-ment tundra with almost zero movement, and granted that one could almost place surveillance on every resident, even so, the land is too large, the whiteouts too frequent, the rivers too wide and deep to prevent even a moderately well-financed and supplied guerilla pro-gram from completely disrupting the security of supply that is essential to electricity sales contracts—let alone financing!

We are unused to thinking this way in North America. We have been lucky.

ROC should have no truck with such ideas, as I noted in Chapter 5 and will elaborate later. But some will want to. Such schemes will be ineffective if denied a safe ROC base of operations, but that very denial will take an act of political courage, as is understood all too well in Dublin and Belfast.

The boundary question, alas, does not end at Ungava. We have yet to deal with Labrador and the South Shore.

No Quebec government has ever formally accepted the British Privy Council decision (back in the days when our final court of appeal was in London) on the boundary between Quebec and Labrador. Quebec will not raise this, but Newfoundland should. This should be one tiny component of the price of a deal.

Far more important to Newfoundland is the matter of Churchill Falls power, now under contract at historically very low rates for another 22 years, with an option to renew for another 25 years on previously agreed terms. The current market rate for such power is immensely higher. If Quebec wants to open the Canadian deal, other matters will be tabled by ROC. This should be one of them.

Of course, this is not just a Newfoundland question. Newfoundland is supported by large annual transfers from Canada every year—and while these may or may not continue after Quebec leaves, anything that can be done in the negotiations to lessen the need will be helpful.

The issue of the South Shore of the St. Lawrence River is tied into the matter of a "land bridge" to the Maritimes after separation. A minimum position for ROC would be to require guarantees of rights of "innocent passage," without fee or hindrance, to land traffic between the Atlantic and Ontario. The same position would apply to the St. Lawrence Seaway, and of course, the language must be sufficiently clear that fabricated events such as bogus "strikes" of lock-tenders do not allow the holding of Ontario to ransom. ROC negotiators will find that Quebec will be perfectly willing to grant unconditional and perpetual rights of passage, by land and by sea. Anything else makes no sense; anything less is unacceptable. The Maritimes need not fear "abandonment" in that sense.

The larger matter of actual territory for ROC on the South Shore will be handled in the recommendations section of this chapter.

Currency is the second major issue. This is far more complex in a technical sense, but easier in fact and emotion.

There has been a great deal written on this matter. David Laidler has produced what is probably the most readable text for most of us.[43] The bottom line is that money matters, and the cooperation of ROC will be useful to Quebec, though not essential.

It is a bargaining point of some importance, on which Canada holds most of the cards. Since Quebec can always adopt a new unit of currency

---

43   "Money After Meech," C.D. Howe Institute Commentary, September 1990, and *Two Nations, One Money*, by David E. W. Laidler and William B. P. Robson, C.D. Howe Institute, 1991, issue no. 3 in "The Canada Round: A Series on the Breakup of Canada."

(the "Parizeau"?) pegged to the United States dollar, it has other options. This option is more costly for them, and probably for ROC as well.

Further down the line, should ROC split up, we may *all* be looking at either a vastly restructured Bank of (former) Canada or joining the United States dollar club. None of this will lead to big changes for any of us, as long as we don't end up with a central bank less responsible than that which we have now. This is important, for surely whatever integrity our currency now has left is due to the Bank of Canada and the private sector, and is despite the worst efforts of all levels of government.

The federal debt is a much tougher issue. It is absolutely enormous—over *half a trillion* dollars, just at the federal level. The joint federal-provincial debt of Canada now approaches the level of the total Gross Domestic Product (GDP), which is the total value of all the work we do collectively in the entire country over a full year. The total net indebtedness of Canadians to foreigners is now well in excess of $300 billion. And we have to borrow about $125 million *per day* at the federal level, or about $70 million *per day* as a country from foreigners, just to maintain our standard of living.

Clearly this cannot continue. Equally clearly, if it is stopped involuntarily and/or abruptly, it will be extremely painful. Thus, as we approach this subject as Canadians, united by the chains of debt whatever our political wishes may be, we either have to keep our creditors happy or suffer an immediate and profound decline in our standard of living. This is a very, very serious question.

To put it in the terms of your average person who has a mortgage approximating a year's salary, it is like worrying about qualifying to refinance the mortgage. If it is not successfully done, you and the family lose the house. You won't starve to death, but your lifestyle will be terribly changed. And to continue an applicable part of the analogy, if the mortgage has been supported by a two-income family that is about to split up, the refinancing negotiations don't get any easier.

And that applies for every Canadian, except for the wealthy or those who live off foreign assets—for at least 95 percent of us, in other words. This applies to *you*. This is not some theoretical "deficit" trumpeted in the headlines at each budget, which never seems to make much difference to ordinary lives. Mishandling of the debt issue by Quebec or ROC will affect just about everyone, in both jurisdictions. No civil servant will be immune—all will take pay cuts, many will lose their jobs. No welfare recipient will be immune—allowances will be slashed. There will be no choice. No business, no union, no doctor, lawyer, or Indian chief will escape the truly savage consequences resulting from a failure on this issue.

The machinery, the mechanisms, the much higher interest rates and much lower dollar—all of these things make interesting reading, but the bottom line is clear. The individual citizem will have less cash—*much* less cash to spend on things other than taxes and mortgage interest—and no one really knows how to calculate this, but it will be perhaps 10 percent less on average in real terms if we get no new foreign loans and investment is pulled out—and this means a lot of pain. And a lot of people will be trampled on as the more powerful scramble to maintain their positions.

This disaster scenario is not unavoidable, but it will take a lot of care and cooperation in a very difficult and highly charged climate. And of course there are two parts to the problem. One is the penalty if we bungle the debt issue. That will be a very high charge. But even if we handle that part successfully, the old order is over.

If Quebec does separate and ROC fragments or just reorganizes, that of itself will be the trigger to immediately take the tough financial measures that would have been needed even had Canada stayed together. The attraction of doing it together is that these tough measures would be planned, voluntary, more fairly distributed as to impact, and much less in total pain. This is a goal worth working for, although to be realistic, we have not seen any sign of this happening voluntarily at the federal level.

Dividing the debt

In looking at the burden of the federal debt, there are only three boxes to put it in. One is labelled "Quebec," one is labelled "ROC" (or its parts), and one is labelled "Default." In the international financial history of the past decade, a surprising number of debts have gone into the

"Default" box, and if that happens, life goes on. But it is not life as before, and I therefore assume we will try to avoid it.

In dividing the debt between the "ROC" and "Quebec" boxes, one must look both at fairness and at clout—fairness first.

Quebec has 25 percent of the population of Canada. To most people, therefore, a 25-75 split would seem to be a good place to start. Indeed there is a famous quote of Jacques Parizeau, speaking in Toronto in late 1990, in which, on the subject of dividing the debt, he forecast that "we will . . . haggle for a few weeks before we come to something like a quarter."

Alas, that was then, and this is now. Mr. Parizeau has not been so categorical since, but the Bélanger-Campeau Commission studies done for the (then Liberal) Quebec government came up with a very different number—17.5 percent of the debt, to be precise, taking into account pension fund liabilities. So the difference of opinion starts at something in the order of $40 billion. This is worth a bit of haggling, in Mr. Parizeau's words. (Viewed another way, this is "just" the amount of this year's federal deficit, which shows the trouble we are in.)

Others in ROC, who take a different approach based on dividing the debt on the basis of where the money has actually been spent over the years, arrive at the very different view that the fair share of Quebec is not in fact just 25 percent, but closer to 31 percent.[44]

"Clout"—ROC versus Quebec

As the process unfolds, we will hear more of these arcane debates than we will really care to. In the end, it will all come down to clout, and not all of the clout resides in Canada. Readers will recall that Hydro-Quebec's financial foundation, and the balance of trade of an independent Quebec, rests on exports of electricity to the eastern United States. Most of Canada's foreign-held debt is either held in or channelled through that same area. The Americans are by no means as desperate

---

44   Paul Boothe and Richard Harris, *Alternative Divisions of Federal Assets and Liabilities*, 1991.

for Quebec power as was the case a decade ago. Indeed, proposed contracts are being cancelled. That is real clout.

An independent Quebec has to have access to capital markets in order to build its dream of a nation. It also must have access to those electricity markets. It will have neither on reasonable terms if it is perceived to have stiffed the creditors in New York. This fact is a part of the leverage of ROC.

ROC has forms of other clout as well, even without employing any of the aggressive tactics canvassed earlier. The world will be *much* easier for Quebec with ROC's cooperation, in myriad details of trade and international relations. This cooperation will no doubt be absolutely contingent on Quebec accepting its share, which will mean close to 25 percent of the debt. It would be very useful for everyone to publicly acknowledge that now, as Mr. Parizeau did once in Toronto in 1990. This alone would have a calming effect on the already nervous international capital markets, which would help Quebec more than it would anyone else.

ROC should make this transparently clear during the course of any independence referendum called in Quebec. It is exceedingly important that this be done because Quebeckers have been misled in this area. The most important political consequence of the Bélanger-Campeau calculation with respect to Quebec's share of the debt does not relate to the level of the debt itself. Rather, based on this finding, the Commission calculated that an independent Quebec would be able to carry on with almost no adverse taxation nor social spending consequences for Quebeckers. At a reasonable debt level, those comfortable calculations go out the window. This may not shift the balance of the vote, but it should be known, and the spokespersons for ROC during the referendum—presumably those in Ottawa, but usefully backed up by provincial representatives—should be absolutely hard and clear on this fact.

Returning to the negotiations, of course Quebec is not without clout. It could simply repudiate *any* share of the debt, saying it belongs to Canada, and that is that. This course of action would mean walking away from a $125 billion obligation; the price would be much international disapproval, active sanctions from ROC, and a host of other unpleasantries. Then, in due course, it would gradually make peace with the world, but it would take a long time. On the other hand, $125 billion is a lot of money.

This course by Quebec, however, would have serious pains for ROC as well. We would be left with 100 percent of the already onerous debt, with a considerably smaller tax base to pay it. Then ROC would have to start thinking itself about repudiating, say, 25 percent (or Quebec's share) of the debt, and telling creditors to ask Quebec City for the balance. This would be messy, and it would certainly exacerbate the already fissiparous tendencies in ROC.

At that point it becomes tempting for British Columbia for example, to say, "we are voluntarily assuming 12 percent (the population share) of the debt of the old Canada, and we're out of here." The alternative is not only the traditional drag of the rest of the country on B.C., but also a new debt burden effectively increased by about 33 percent by the default of Quebec, plus—and worst of all—continued association with what would certainly be a nation in misery and turmoil.

Trade is the final issue we deal with here, and only briefly, despite its importance. Quebec and Ontario sell each other more than $20 billion of goods and services each year, and that is a major fact. Moreover, Quebec sells almost $30 billion of goods and services into international markets every year, primarily that of the United States.[45]

Efficient trade requires a known and stable legal climate—not just of duties and tariffs, but also of commercial law, and such mundane things as enforcing contracts across boundaries. We are used to a particular way of doing such things, and the required changes would be very complex and time consuming, even with the best of good will on each side. Separation would, therefore, break many of these links pending renegotiation, and that takes time, even with good will. The famous "business as usual" slogan of the separatists simply will not happen—at least not without the cooperation of ROC.

The thing to be emphasized about trade for the purposes of this discussion is that almost all of the negotiating clout runs in favour of ROC. It is in ROC's interest to reach rapid and reasonable arrangements

---

45   Statistics Canada, *The Daily*, August 24, 1993.

with respect to trade—that is quite true. But the pain of reaching these arrangements slowly, or not at all, is far more severe for Quebec. Cooperation in trade matters is, therefore, a major bargaining lever, and even discussions among reasonable people sometimes need such levers to make progress.

Under this general rubric of trade, one must mention the matter of head offices in Montreal. That the head offices of such corporations as Air Canada and CN Rail would be removed is clear, for the majority ownership will remain in ROC under any kind of settlement. Other entities funded by Canada, such as the Space Research Institute and a long list of others, would disappear, probably mostly into smoke rather than somewhere else. Many private head offices might also move, though in truth the exodus to Toronto is so well advanced that this would be much less important than it was even ten years ago.

Recommendations

In summary, then, on the issues, here are the views of this book.

Boundaries are by far the most important and emotional issue for Quebeckers. This is also emotional for many residents of ROC, but it does not carry the quite the same level of intensity. Indeed, in my opinion, as long as our moral obligations are looked after, it would be silly to worry about changing boundaries. What interest have we in James Bay-Ungava? If the rights of minorities now protected by Canada are given proper guarantees (and enforceable by sanctions) by Quebec, that should be the end of it. In such circumstances, ROC will only seriously raise boundary issues in negotiations, or in the smallest way cooperate with those who would do so, if and only if it is looking for a very messy divorce. This is not in our interest.

The *quid pro quo* will be permanent and include absolutely free passage to the Atlantic, a fair deal on Churchill Falls power for New-foundland, and confirmation of Labrador's boundaries.

Currency and **Trade** are extremely complex technical issues that can be resolved by good will, and will carry more dangers for Quebec than for ROC, while giving more bargaining clout to ROC than Quebec.

The federal debt is an extremely dangerous issue. It must be handled rapidly, forcefully, and unambiguously by *both* parties unless both sides want to risk a great deal of pain. Indeed—and we should all muse upon this—it is really essential that the matter of the debt be resolved in principle immediately upon the election of a separatist government in Quebec. Background talks should be underway on that topic right now, most desirably convened in utmost secrecy by the Bank of Canada and without the formal authority of any government. The Bank is responsible for the currency, and this issue lies at the heart of its mandate. Clearly, any binding agreements will have to await a referendum and negotiations thereafter, but the security of our creditors should not be in doubt at any point of the process or we will all pay for it heavily.

If and when it comes to this, the negotiations with Quebec will not be easy. The choice under joint control—mostly the control of ROC, as the stronger party—is whether the negotiations will be rational and relatively serene, or a horror show that takes over our national consciousness for years.

We truly do not need the latter development. While the terms of separation with Quebec will be important, the far greater business of our own relationships within ROC is what should capture most of our attention. Quebec issues have driven our agenda for too long. Once independence is decided upon, it will be time for the rest of us to rearrange our *own* lives, and put most of our energy there.

Chapter 8:
Stuck Together or Disassembled—Pieces of the ROC

THERE IS A MODERN FOLK-SAYING we should touch on at the outset of this chapter—"If it ain't broke, don't fix it!" Maybe that was true of Canada pre-Meech Lake. Maybe it was even true in 1993, though I would question that. But if Quebec leaves, there is no doubt—it's broke! It's time to fix it.

But once a decision is made to fundamentally rethink *any* organization, whether it be business, social, or political, there is no way of knowing in advance where the re-examination may lead and where the change may stop. Politicians are very aware and very wary of this. That is why in Canada, we make sure that our occasional fundamental rethinkings are done by Royal Commissions, which have no power to actually *do* anything. That is why American politicians over the more than two centuries of their country's existence have vigorously opposed attempts to make constitutional changes through the machinery of Constitutional Conventions.

Although the U.S. Constitution provides for such a device, the professional politician's nightmare is a so-called "runaway convention," convened for one purpose but ending up by rooting around in every part of the basic law and making serious changes. Politicians, especially those in power, like the established order. And why not? It got them where they are.

Like it or not, a decision by Quebec to separate will trigger just that kind of fundamental review of the entire structure of the old Canada. And very much up for many people's consideration will be the question of whether other provincial parts of Queen Victoria's 1867 creation should also go back to where they came from, so to speak. The pressures for this tendency are explained by theory, by empirical evidence, and by the process we will be in.

Theory of Canada undermined

The theory is this: Canada, as we have known it, is a balanced and functioning whole. If Quebec departs, the balance will be very fundamentally changed.

The balance between *rich and poor* regions will be changed. No longer will the small provinces of the Atlantic have a politically muscular friend in the form of Quebec to assist in levering basically unconditional largesse—and huge amounts of it—from the better-off regions. That "given" of the old Canada will be endangered, and will probably be gone.

The balance between *centralists and decentralists* will be changed. No longer will British Columbia and Alberta have that same politically muscular friend to resist the centralizing tendencies of Ottawa, strongly backed by the Atlantic, Saskatchewan/Manitoba and Ontario, each for their own good reasons. B.C. and Alberta won't like that. They *already* don't like it, even with the assistance they currently have in these matters from Quebec. (There is very definitely a natural alliance between these three provinces in many things. It is an alliance of which we may see more before the confusion is over.)

The balance between East and West will be changed. While the myth that westerners are closer in kind to western Americans than to eastern Canadians is just that, a myth,[46] there are nevertheless major

---

46   The common political elements among Canadians of collective social action and commitment to an orderly and managed society are stronger than are

differences in approach to the world, as the most cursory examination of the politics of the various regions will reveal. The West simply couldn't agree to having ROC dominated by central Canada in the old way, and yet by numbers Ontario would be entitled to be even *more* dominant.

If the balance is knocked askew, so is the other element of our balanced and functioning whole: the "functioning" part. The most obvious fact is that with Quebec gone, ROC would be physically disconnected. One may take some comfort from the distance of the "Lower 48" from Alaska, but the fact is still important. Geography matters, and has mattered throughout history.

Many of the linkages of trade would be broken. We have already noted that the huge two-way trade of over $20 billion per year between Ontario and Quebec would be disrupted. This disruption would be equally true of Quebec and the Atlantic and, for other reasons, of Ontario and the Atlantic. (Neither the Atlantic nor Quebec trade much with the West in any case.)

Many of the linkages of custom would be broken. We spoke in an earlier chapter about the impact on attitudes toward multi-culturalism, aboriginal relations, "Canadian culture," and immigration. The already very fragile accommodations on all these sensitive areas would be jiggled and probably broken in an unbalanced ROC.

Given the above, there are certainly adequate theoretical reasons to be rather certain that the whole affair *should* be up for review, even if inertia were strong enough to avoid that for a short period. The long run strains would surface, and they might as well surface now.

Pressure from the West

The empirical reasons to believe that a re-examination of ROC is inevitable are just now starting to show up, especially in British Columbia. The evidence is so far unscientific, circumstantial, and anecdotal, but it is accumulating.

---

our political similarities to Americans. Whether this common view guarantees a single country is another question, however.

The first exhibit is the surprising success of the Reform Party in B.C. in the federal election of October 1993. Reform did better in B.C. than it did even in its home base of Alberta. More to the point, Reform was supported in B.C. for importantly different reasons.

Alberta is a conservative province. There are just no two ways about that. Since the Progressive Conservatives refused to be conservative in fact rather than merely in name, Reform was the way to go for Alberta for ideological as well as regional reasons. This was the major theme, along with a strong minor theme of protest.

British Columbia, to the contrary, did *not* vote for Reform because it is a conservative province, which it is not. It is more of a populist/protest province, though this is changing with the underlying demographics of in-migration from Canada and abroad. In B.C., protest against the Ottawa system was the major theme, the conservative motives being less important. It would be wrong to make too much of this difference between the two provinces, and indeed it may turn out to be only a difference in timing. For the moment though, B.C. is clearly the most alienated province of ROC, *vis-à-vis* the federal setup.

This sentiment appeared in the runup to the Charlottetown Accord, when B.C. not only led the opposition to this quintessentially Ottawa compromise, but also voted most strongly to reject it. It recently appeared in the very heated reaction to an apparent intent by Ottawa to cheat B.C. out of two new seats in the Commons that have been earned by population growth. My sense is that few in B.C. really care about two more seats, because no one really thinks Ottawa is ever going to be very helpful to B.C. It is the insult, the symbol that rankles.

The empirical evidence is showing up, as well, in private conversations in B.C., where people routinely debate a question that would have been totally unmentionable just a few years ago, namely, "If Quebec goes, should we go too?"

On April 29, 1994, the open-liner Rafe Mair devoted his entire three hour program to taking calls on this very question. (One wonders if the CRTC knows this!) Answers were put in the following categories:

- stay with the rest of Canada
- go it alone
- go it with Alberta

- unite with "Canada West"[47]

When the smoke cleared after a rather vigorous program which included about 60 calls, almost half the votes were captured by simple independence for B.C., followed by the Canada West option. "Stay with the rest of Canada" got less than 20 percent of the votes.

This is extremely interesting. One must make many reservations in interpreting such data—small sample, self-selected audience, and so on—but there are other facets too. Almost every caller stated how glad he or she was that this subject was finally being raised. There was relatively little emotion on the subject, given its cataclysmic character, but views were firm and people clearly understood the importance of what they were talking about.

Another note of interest is that only one caller suggested that B.C. should join the United States. It is curious how widespread the assumption is that joining the U.S. is the "natural" thing for fragments of Canada to do. Disregarding what the Americans would think of taking on any given piece from the Atlantic to the Pacific, it is quite clear that British Columbians would have no interest in the idea. On the one hand, it would mean giving up many things we hold dear, starting with Medicare and many other of our Canadian-style social programs. Even if these could somehow be preserved and funded (by a Washington, D.C. not used to giving states their way, nor the cash to do it), there are other elements B.C. does not need, gun laws being a minor example. Survey data over the years have confirmed this lack of interest.[48]

Two B.C. MLAs, one Independent, the other of the Progressive Democratic Alliance (things are complicated in B.C., with five opposition groups in the Legislature), have made statements on the topic. The PDA spokesman, former Liberal Leader Gordon Wilson, has said that B.C. separation, plain and simple, is a respectable option, if the province

---

47   Mair did not initially include "Canada West" as an option because of his opinion that this arrangement might just give us a smaller version of the problems of entanglement and federalism we are now finding with Canada. Enough callers insisted on this as an option that it was added.

48   Published work by the Angus Reid organization indicates only about 4 percent of British Columbians find this an attractive option.

is pushed. Wilson had a stormy history as a party leader, but he has one of the best political noses in the province. And David Mitchell, an Independent (former Liberal) and a most respected MLA in the Legislature, has said, "if our confederation is torn apart by Quebec's possible separation, we will need to reconsider our citizenship. . . . And in my view, we will need to put British Columbia first."

"Who do you put first, your province or your country?" is one of those litmus tests that is supposed to elicit an automatic "My country!" response. This hasn't been true in Quebec for a long time. In fact in a December 1993 Gallup poll, 49 percent of Quebeckers saw themselves as Quebeckers first, as opposed to 38 percent who answered "Canadian." The sentiment is now rapidly changing in B.C. Even though the same Gallup poll saw 60 percent of British Columbians answering "Canadian," 13 percent said they were provincials first, and 23 percent said "both," which is a weasely answer that really says something like "Probably provincial but not quite ready to say it." When Gallup asked a very similar question described in their release of August 13, 1991, British Columbians' "primary allegiance" to Canada was 9 points higher. These are small straws in the wind, but interesting ones.

So there is at least some growing empirical evidence that if Quebec leaves, the established order of ROC will be questioned, at least from the westernmost province. Of course, as in the Charlottetown Accord, once this sort of a tide starts running, it spreads.

The Quebec deal as a model for ROC

And finally on this initial inquiry as to whether the basics of ROC are likely to be deeply questioned, consider what our negotiators from the last chapter will be doing as they work out the arrangements with Quebec's representatives. They will be defining an appropriate relationship between Quebec and ROC, yes, but in effect, they will also be designing a pattern *for any other part of the old Canada to relate to the rest.*

So this illustrates the process argument: with only minor modifications required, an acceptable deal with Quebec also sets the parameters for an acceptable deal with B.C., or Alberta, or any other province or region that might have parting thoughts. Quebec separation in effect will force the invention of a secession protocol for everyone. This unintended result would certainly not have been part of anyone's plan, but the roadmap will be there, right on the table. The debt formula? Common market and other trade questions? Currency? The pattern for each will be there.

Of course, there could be additional elements in a partition of ROC, based on different emotions. For example, there could be no question of equalization continuing for Quebec, but it is quite conceivable that an independent Ontario, Alberta, and British Columbia might want, as part of the terms of dissociation from ROC, to voluntarily provide for a stream of (declining) adjustment payments to the Atlantic, to cushion the transition. There is clearly a general feeling of good will between most parts of Canada, and a breakup agreement might well reflect that.

In summary, for all of the above reasons—theoretical-, empirical-, and process-related—there is every reason to believe that we will have to get into a fundamental re-examination of ROC, if Quebec goes, and that its continuity cannot be taken for granted. Of course, neither can its breakup. The status quo has always been the first consideration of our minds, and what is left of Canada, minus Quebec, will be the status quo after independence, truncated House of Commons, Peace Tower, Governor-General, and all. This is very much one of the options to be weighed. The point here is that it is not the *only* one, as has usually been assumed. Most of us just haven't taken the time to think about anything else.

The next two jobs then are, first, to define the issues for consideration, and, second, to propose machinery for facilitating the discussion and decision-making that will be required.

Defining the issues for ROC

To define the issues, let us ask: "what do we want our governments to do?" Once we have the answer to that question, the next one is, "How do we best organize our governmental structures to get those things done?"[49]

Government tasks (all levels included):

- Establish and maintain peace and order within our territory
- Provide for a climate of stability and predictability under a rule of law
- Provide a means for the constitution of the state to change with changing times
- Provide a means for citizens to be appropriately involved in their governance, with the means to require accountability
- Conduct the necessary military and diplomatic relations with the outside world to protect our domestic society and advance our world-wide objectives
- Establish standards, regulations, infrastructure, and legal structures for the orderly pursuit of private objectives within a rule of law
- Provide for a stable currency
- Provide for a sharing of our collective income to establish minimum safety nets
- Provide for timely and trusted dispute-resolution machinery
- Establish or provide for development and conservation of resources, including human resources, natural resources, and the environment
- preserve or enhance valued collective resources such as culture and language

That's really about it, and it is a list that can be agreed upon by almost all in the political spectrum, from right to left. The arguments turn around such practical details as "How much will it cost?" "Who pays?" "Private or public delivery of services? Private or public infra-

---

49 An alternative approach would be to list all the departments and agencies of all levels of government and see how best to sort them out. This has a practical usefulness, and we will get to a version of this, but it overlooks some basic aspects.

structure?" The job then becomes one of assigning these tasks to the appropriate government unit, and getting on with it.

Note that these tasks are largely ends, rather than means, which is one reason that agreement is so easy. The questions as to whether a safety net should include Medicare, with or without user fees, or whether an overarching Charter is the best way to secure justice, and matters such as these are left to each jurisdiction, each generation, each elected government to work out over its own time span. Constitution-building begins with very broad bricks, on which rest the more moveable Lego blocks of daily governance.

Rules for assigning tasks

In Canada, and in many other countries like ours, we have come to the conclusion that the size of the country and the variety of the conditions make a good case for the division of labour between governments. That is a main principle of *federalism*—the idea that different jobs can usefully be done by different levels of government.[50] Once again, the main argument is not about principle, but about details—exactly *which* level should do exactly *what*?

In our country, we have raised this to an art form. We have three (and often four) levels of government stepping on each other's toes. We have agencies and commissions and crown corporations in the act. We have overlap and duplication and constant negotiation, even within one level of government, let alone among several. It is all very expensive, and the actual pay-cheques and expense accounts are only the start of it.

The cost of having the best, or at least the most important, minds in the country constantly engaged in sterile, jurisdictional debate is incalculable. The barrier to getting on with business, imposed by the complexities of our system is equally large. It is not unlike tax law, which

---

50   Another idea of great importance is that the division of powers between governments helps to secure the liberty of the people. Federalism is one of the truly great inventions of political history, even if our version has had problems.

engages some of our finest legal brains in fundamentally unproductive pursuits and often drives foolishly uneconomic decisions on the basis of tax matters.

It is not that jurisdictional questions are not important—of course they are, just as is tax law. But there comes a point where overemphasis on these issues ceases to serve the general public, serving only the inmates of the system itself. (Legislatures have been described as the only asylums where the inmates make the rules. This has some truth, as anyone who has been there would admit. They are small, mad worlds of their own.)

Let us return to the Toynbee argument that a national state is no more than a public utility. We have no compunction in insisting that our public utilities be efficient in the exercise of their duties. Quebec or no Quebec, have we not yet reached the point where we should re-examine our governments from this point of view?

That re-examination should start on the basis of principles we can all buy into. Here are the basic few.

The first principle is *subsidiarity*, the ten-dollar word used by the European Union to describe a very simple idea. The concept is this: whenever there is a task to be done, it should be done by the entity equipped to do it that is closest to the people, taking into consideration all factors, including customer satisfaction. And when there is a doubt as to which level of government is best able to do a job, the benefit of the doubt should go to the smallest or lowest level unit. In other words, all things being equal (which they never are), community groups are better decision-makers and service-providers than municipalities, which are better than provinces, which are better than the feds.

It will not take long for anyone involved in the commerce or politics of this country to draw up a quick hit list for the useful application of this idea.

The second principle is *decentralization*. This principle says, for example, that even if a large government is the best organization to have responsibility for something, actual operational decisions should nevertheless be decentralized to local offices which understand local conditions. There is always a tradeoff between large-scale consistency and precedent, and local conditions requiring a variation from standard.

"Consistency is the hobgoblin of little minds," said Ralph Waldo Emerson, yet on the other side of the street lies anarchy. Life is a balance.

The third principle is *viability*. A government charged with a responsibility must be large enough to survive while carrying it out, at a very minimum. This would seem to be a simple test to pass in Canada, given that little Prince Edward Island, with its population of 130,000, has survived as a province. But if the approximately 38 percent of its budgetary revenue[51] provided by Ottawa were withdrawn, would P.E.I. be viable as a province? Perhaps it would be viable more as a regional centre, or as a mere district of a new, merged province of Atlantica.[52] Of course, we can afford anything we are willing to pay for. What about the Islanders? Hard questions indeed. We must ask them.

Viability is above all a financial test, in Canadian terms. In less fortunate parts of the world, it is a military test as well. With the effective protection of our neighbour to the south, we don't need the military dimension, except for our self-respect. This is a good thing, as we are unwilling to pay for it.

Viability is also a function of *will*. Israel, tiny in size and in population, and surrounded by mortal enemies, has made a go of it. One must acknowledge the phenomenal infusion of American dollars and weapons to help it pass the previously-mentioned tests, but the key element for Israel has been will. ROC is missing an important point if it overlooks the element of will in Quebec. An economy that looks like a loser can be transformed into a winner by the belief and efforts of its people. But it is damned hard work.

The fourth principle is *diversification*, or *reach*. This relates partly to the concept of portfolio diversification, where risk is reduced (as is return) by having a basket of assets which are not too likely to all go wrong (or right) at the same time. Since most humans hate unexpected losses and downsides much more than they love unexpected payoffs, risk reduction makes sense. You would not want to have an economy

51   P.E.I. Budget, 1994/95.

52   It is too bad that the name "Atlantis" is associated with sinking under the sea, for the lost-continent moniker is a lovely word.

based only on grain if you could have oil and manufacturing in the mix as well. If you can add a software development industry, so much the better. That is the first part of diversification.

The second part is equally important. You need a mix of different things to foster the synergy of human creativity. It is one thing to have an arm of government doing something terribly important and totally dull, like making sure the sewers are working. But you also need to do a few more interesting things in order to attract the kind of people you want to run your public business. Fortunately, government is so inherently complicated and fascinating that this is more of a theoretical problem. But the same principle also applies to the wider community, where a mix of peoples and views often leads to good results. (Of course it can also cause friction, but does Japan work better because it is homogeneous?)

The fifth principle is *minimum complexity*.[53] The KISS injunction (Keep It Simple, Stupid) has a lot of merit when one is dealing with millions of people, all busy with their own lives. It is worth giving up a certain amount—or even quite a lot—of theoretical efficiency if the tradeoff is that the system is understood by the public it serves. Democratic systems only work well if the guidance system works, and that depends upon some minimal public understanding.

The sixth principle is a proper joining of *responsibility and authority*. "Authority," of course, also means financial resources, in this context. This juxtaposition is essential if we are to have proper accountability, which is really essential in "governing the government." You have to be able to hold some entity responsible for doing or not doing the right thing.

It is interesting to note how these principles relate to each other on the matter of the desirable size of a governmental unit. Subsidiarity and minimum complexity push for smaller sizes. Viability and diversifica-

---

53   This is not to argue with the aphorism, advanced by one-time federal minister Don Jamieson of Newfoundland that "the denial of complexity is the essence of tyranny." He was quite right. But bafflegab and untraceable responsibility arising out of complexity are the essence of another kind of tyranny.

tion may push one up the numbers scale, but not necessarily. For example, it is quite possible to have a very large common market that provides the desired economic diversification, while keeping most governmental powers at a local level. Decentralization and the responsibility/authority mix are pretty much neutral on size. Indeed, even though it is easier to achieve accountability in a smaller unit, that unit may not have the necessary resources to really be held accountable, so there is a balancing act.

One other matter on size, having to do with our modern world, is important. As our world becomes globalized, corporations trans-national, culture more homogenized and universal, cities larger, and individuals more interchangeable in this enormous machine, people have come more and more to feel the problem of *identity*. A smaller, slower world, where one has more stability and continuity in relationships with others, helps provide an antidote. Thus, it is not surprising that we see people being driven or retreating back to smaller groups— their families, their religions, their ethnic communities, their neighbourhoods—all of this has to do with identity.

At the level of politics, this return to tradition clearly argues for smaller, more homogeneous units. Writ somewhat larger, it is a key to the forces driving Quebec. The old Quebec could protect its identity much more easily without the incessant pressure of modern transportation and communications. No more. That identity is under threat like so many others,[54] and we anglos might understand it better if we thought of some of the threats to identity in our own lives, be they the power of American culture, the perceived decay in values in the modern world, or the loss of the kind of society where we didn't have to lock our doors. There is natural tendency to want to think a bit smaller, a bit slower, and we must take that into account.

Once again, that's about it. The concepts are not complicated. And the instructions for this particular nation-state assembly kit have built-in simplifying procedures, of which subsidiarity and KISS are the most

---

54 But whatever the strains from outside media sources, note the wise insight of Peter Desbarats in *René* (Lévesque) as to how television helped shape and define modern Quebec.

important. Science students will recall Occam's Razor. This principle says that if you have several possible explanations for an observation, choose the simplest one. It is a good approach for constitution-building as well.

How the current Canada stacks up

The current Canada performs all the tasks required of governments, and does most of them fairly well. Except for two failures, one of which may prove fatal, our governments have done not badly. We are relatively peaceful and economically comfortable as far as this world goes, and we are improving in most areas of human welfare as we understand it. Among our various levels of government, things are handled, though perhaps inefficiently, at too high a cost. But there are those two failures.

The first is our determination to consume at a distinctly higher level than that which we earn. We "want it all," as they say, but we don't want to work *quite* that hard, eh? We want governments to fix this and that and every other problem, but we don't want to pay the taxes to make that possible. So we borrow. The political process shifts the burden to the taxpayers of the future—if we can find enough of them!

We have been borrowing at tremendous, staggering, unsustainable rates. In the great sweep of history this does not matter, as reality has a way of asserting itself in due course, and the cure is more or less painful depending upon whether or not the patient is foresighted and cooperative. Financial reality always comes one way or another, and it will come to Canada. That is not the fatal problem; it merely hurts.

However, the financial position we have gotten ourselves into means that we have no flexibility to solve our other big problem by throwing dollars at it. The other big problem is that powerful groups just don't like the system any more. Those groups are Quebeckers, natives, and increasingly, westerners. Each of these contingents could have found a lot of charm in the principles of subsidiarity, decentralization, minimum complexity, and accountability had they been applied at the right time. They were not.

Yet the changing modern world has rolled on, and the pressures have led regions and groups to look for solutions through running their own show. The "third order of government" concept of natives is just like the Quebec search for independence, translated into the context of natives in Canada. Lacking a territorial base, they have sought a legal construct in which to do the same thing.

The West's push for a Triple-E Senate will one day be seen as an early version of the same ambition—for westerners to get more control over their own lives through the means of getting more control over the central government.

Provincial governments have never much liked the Senate reform idea. This has been partly because it would weaken their own legitimacy, and also because their own bureaucratic folk wisdom over many years has taught provincial governments that the only way to really control things at home is to have the power at home. People are slowly coming to see that a successful Triple-E Senate would really increase the power and centralization of Ottawa, as it has done in Washington, D.C.

For whatever reasons, our system has shown itself incapable of dealing with these tensions to date. If Quebec defeats its referendum, there may be a chance to try again. This book assumes that the referendum will pass. And so we move on to discuss how ROC or its fragments might fare.

Viability of ROC and its components

In talking about viability, one should start by defining terms, for in the sense of mere survival at some lower standard of living, every province of Canada could subsist on its own. This would not be true in some other parts of the world, where dissolution would bring military threats from acquisitive neighbours. The presence of the benign giant to the south shields the elements of ROC from such concerns.

But surely mere survival is not what most Canadians today would want to call a "viable" option. Even our so-called "poverty line," as defined by Statistics Canada, is so far above the level of mere survival, that we would see levels of income and a living standard that most would say are just plain unacceptable if any region got down to that survival level on average. "Viable," therefore, means being able to provide a standard of living at something not very much worse than that of today in any given area, though quantifying this is up to each individual.

Viability will also require meeting two other tests. A viable unit will need to have the ability to service its ongoing debt. For the purposes of this analysis, each region would be assigned its own debt, of course, plus its *per capita* share of the federal debt.

In addition, each unit will have to be viable in the sense of maintaining a healthy balance of payments: it must sell as much to the outside world as it buys, less any new borrowing it might be able to do.

As we proceed through the list, we will see that some arrangements are not "viable" by one or more of these tests. That does not mean that these wrenching political developments—such as that of an Atlantic region off on its own in a cold world—could not happen. It just means that if they *do* happen, or as they become probable, the non-viable regions will have to adjust, through some mix of offensive and defensive strategies. Even the defensive parts are not easy: out-migration, subsidy from the richer partners of the old ROC for a time, or even possibly association with the United States. And the trouble with out-migration strategy is that while it may solve problems for those individuals, their departure leaves behind an even higher per capita debt.

The offensive strategy is a lot harder work, though not necessarily tougher in the long run. This is essentially survival by becoming more productive. A larger percentage of the population working longer hours for more days of more years is the simple way to do this. Working "smarter," or becoming more efficient, is another way. This may require expensive and scarce capital, but it can also involve low cost approaches as work rules change.

The point is that some regions will be *forced* into such choices if matters unfold in certain ways. Other regions will probably find higher productivity a useful goal in any case, even though they will be "viable" by most measures. Being viable is good, but being poorer is not.

If there is a silver lining in all of this, it is that our financial constraints would push us some distance down this same road to productivity, in any case, if we wished to preserve the existing living standards of the Canada of today.

That said, let us look at the "viability" of the following 7 potential arrangements:[55]

1. ROC continuing as a whole

2. The Atlantic

3. Quebec[56]

4. Ontario

5. Saskatchewan/Manitoba

6. Alberta

7. British Columbia

As the intent is to see how each of these might do on a freestanding basis, alone in the world, each arrangement will be measured on the following bases:

- Current GDP
- GDP adjusted for an end of all federal payments and receipts other than debt service
- The increase or decline in GDP per capita
- Consequent reduction or increase in current consumption
- Current debt (with the federal share apportioned by population)
- Debt compared to current and adjusted GDP figures
- Current debt-servicing charges (with the federal share apportioned by population)
- Balance of trade in goods and services with the rest of the world (defined to include what is currently the rest of Canada)

The underlying assumption of the following presentation is that each of the units listed is "off on its own." That means no more money is sent *to* Ottawa, except to service the population share of the old federal debt. It also means no more money comes *from* Ottawa, except to pay

---

55   To make it easier to follow the tables, we have kept them to the main individual units of analysis. The reader can experiment with various combinations such as Ontario/Manitoba/Saskatchewan, or whatever.

56   Quebec is included in these tables, even though its decision will already have been made by the reference date of this chapter. The data are still of interest for comparative purposes.

interest on that debt to any bondholders in the province(s) under consideration. In other words, from the point of view of each of the units in these tables, Ottawa will have disappeared except for the debt.

In effect, this means two things:

a) an end to net transfer payments as far as each province is concerned, and

b) the end of the federal deficit, as far as each province is concerned.

This is a very harsh scenario. It is equivalent to not only eliminating the federal deficit immediately, but also eliminating equalization and all of the other transfer payments that some provinces rely on and others pay for.

Is this wildly out of touch with what could happen? Not at all. If Canada breaks up, it is exactly what will happen for the poorer provinces. The three rich provinces will do a little better because they may still be able to borrow, if they are on their own. The poorer provinces will be unable to borrow because they won't be able to service their existing debts. And any ongoing "foreign aid" from the richer provinces would likely be small and short-term.

But then, some might say, what about the ROC column? Is this assumption on borrowing not too harsh there? As long as we stick together in ROC, surely we can continue to live off the proceeds of borrowing and retain our inter-regional subsidies? Maybe, but I don't think so. If Quebec splits from Canada, the financial shock, as the international community contemplates what is happening and could happen, and the political tensions in the remaining ROC will act against the continuity of both these debt and transfer policies.

Even today, Canada as a whole doesn't have a whole lot of room left on its credit card, and if and when seriously political instability is demonstrated, there will be even less. There is room to argue that ROC might do a bit better than its column predicts in what follows, but I wouldn't bet on it.

Let us examine the following two tables. The first, table 8.1, calculates what happens with the notional disappearance of Ottawa, from the point of view of each unit. First, we record the current federal tax take in each unit. Then we assume that each unit will take over the debt

Table 8.1: Calculation of New GDP

	Atlantic Provinces	Ont.	Man. + Sask.	Alberta	B.C.	Quebec	ROC
	(Millions of Dollars)						
1. GDP, 1990	$40,877	$273,431	$44,426	$71,408	$81,875	$154,120	$515,116
2. GDP per capita ($)	17,613	28,045	21,296	28,874	26,137	22,771	25,961
3. Total federal taxes, 1990	7,430	53,328	7,569	11,282	15,324	24,473	95,443
4. of which reserved for debt charges[a]	3,718	15,619	3,342	3,962	5,018	10,843	31,787
5. Available for general expenditure (3-4)	3,712	37,709	4,227	7,320	10,306	13,630	63,656
6. Total federal spending	17,815	60,750	11,634	11,002	14,743	35,062	116,691
7. Interest paid to residents	1,958	26,163	1,550	1,902	3,297	7,567	35,063
8. Current general expenditure (6-7)	15,857	34,587	10,084	9,100	11,446	27,495	81,628
9. Required reduction in general expenditure (8-5), 1990	12,145	-3,122	5,857	1,780	1,140	13,865	17,972
10. New GDP (1-9), 1990	28,732	276,553	38,569	69,628	80,735	140,255	497,144
11. New GDP per capita ($), 1990	12,380	28,366	18,489	28,154	25,773	20,723	25,055
12. New GDP, 1994 estimate	32,278	298,928	41,227	76,520	95,883	152,476	550,063

[a]Debt charges are regionally allocated according to population.
Source: *Provincial Outlook, Spring 1994*, Conference Board of Canada, April 14, 1994; *Government Spending Facts 2*, Isabella Horry and Michael Walker, The Fraser Institute, forthcoming 1994.

Table 8.2: Viability Analysis

	Atlantic Provinces	Ont.	Man. + Sask.	Alberta	B.C.	Quebec	ROC
	(Millions of dollars)						
Current GDP, 1994 estimate[a]	45,943	295,553	47,490	78,476	97,237	167,549	570,081
Current GDP per capita, 1994 ($)	19,215	27,247	22,401	29,271	27,018	23,142	26,230
New GDP, 1994 (see table 8.1)	32,278	298,928	41,227	76,520	95,883	152,476	550,063
New GDP per capita, 1994 ($)	13,500	27,559	19,447	28,542	26,642	21,060	25,309
Percentage change of New GDP/capita from Current GDP/capita	-29.7%	1.1%	-13.2%	-2.5%	-1.4%	-9.0%	-3.5%
Required reduction in current consumption (see table 8.1, line 9), 1994	13,665	-3,375	6,236	1,956	1,354	15,073	20,018
Required reduction in current consumption as a percentage of current GDP	29.7%	-1.1%	13.2%	2.5%	1.4%	9.0%	3.5%
Required reduction in current consumption per capita ($)	5,715	-311	2.954	730	376	2,082	921
Total Net Debt, 1994[b]	68,927	298,675	58,503	68,033	86,916	224,229	597,087
Net Debt as a percentage of Current GDP	150.0%	101.1%	123.2%	86.7%	89.4%	133.8%	104.7%

Table 8.2: Viablility Analysis

	Atlantic Provinces	Ont.	Man. + Sask.	Alberta	B.C.	Quebec	ROC
			(Millions of dollars)				
Net Debt as a percentage of New GDP	213.5%	99.9%	141.9%	88.9%	90.6%	147.1%	108.5%
Total Debt Charges[c]	6,193	24,509	6,569	7,231	8,414	17,689	53,173
Debt Charges per capita ($)	2,590	2,260	3,099	2,697	2,338	2,443	2,447
Debt Charges as a percentage of Current GDP	13.5%	8.3%	13.8%	9.2%	8.7%	10.6%	9.3%
Debt Charges as a percentage of New GDP	19.2%	8.2%	15.9%	9.4%	8.8%	11.6%	9.7%
Balance of Trade in Goods & Services with the rest of the world, 1989[d]	-8,177	12,741	-2,090	1,742	-1,719	-4,069	2,090

[a]1994 estimate of GDP is a Conference Board of Canada estimate.
[b]1994 total net debt is estimated by The Fraser Institute. Federal debt is distributed according to population shares.
[c]Debt charges include provincial, local, and federal debt charges. The federal portion is the population share of federal debt charges.
[d]Rest of the world includes provinces which do not form part of the new region.
Source: *The Daily*, August 24, 1993, Statistics Canada; *Public Sector Assets and Liabilities*, cat. 68-508, Statistics Canada, March 1994; *Canadian Economic Observer*, catalogue 11-010, Statistics Canada; data from the Public Institutions Division of Statistics Canada; *Provincial Outlook*, Spring 1994, Conference Board of Canada, April 14 1994; Federal & Provincial budgets, estimates & public accounts; "Inside Canada's Government Debt Problem and the Way Out," Robin Richardson, International Centre for the Study of Public Debt, *Fraser Forum Critical Issues Bulletin*, The Fraser Institute, May 1994; *Government Spending Facts 2*, Isabella Horry and Michael Walker, The Fraser Institute, forthcoming 1994.

service on its population share of the federal debt, just as we will require Quebec to do, and we calculate that amount. The difference between the two figures gives the "federal" tax take in the province that is available for spending on goods and services and people after servicing the debt.

We then continue in that table to list the total federal expenditure in the province under consideration, and we separate out the amount that is received in payment of interest on the old federal debt. Since we have assumed that each unit is still paying to service the debt, we assume as well that the bondholders are getting their interest. It is only the federal expenditure remaining after this calculation that has—in the past—been available for general spending in, or outside on behalf of, the province under consideration.[57]

Now, since each province or region under consideration is "off on its own," all that it has to spend on matters that used to be looked after by Ottawa is its own residual share of taxes formerly collected in the province by Ottawa, after servicing the old debt. The difference between what Ottawa used to spend and what the province can now spend from its own tax base is a measure of how living standards will be affected in the province. From this we calculate a new GDP for the province, which feeds into the next table.

At this point we must emphasize once again that these are very rough, first order approximations. They are not forecasts of how the real world will shake out after trade patterns and multiplier effects and consequent migration and various uncertainty costs and effects are considered. They only point out a direction, but they do tell a very cautionary tale.

As is obvious from table 8.1, these results are very serious for the Atlantic region, Quebec, and Saskatchewan/Manitoba. These figures are integrated with such matters as debt in table 8.2. As well, this table includes measures of implied reductions in consumption and a balance of trade measure for each unit with the "rest of the world," which is defined to include the rest of the old Canada.

---

57   This matter of funds spent outside on the province's behalf has some horrendous consequences for Ottawa, to which we shall return.

The first thing that should be said about these tables is that any given set of numbers provides a very inadequate representation of reality. Some measures could be found to produce more cheerful results than these; others could no doubt be found to do less so. The next thing to be said is that these numbers are produced as if the world stood still. Of course it doesn't, and all these micro-economies would change in very important ways if they were alone in the world.

Even with those two caveats, table 8.2 is exceedingly alarming for much of the country. As one might expect, the change in adjusted GDP and the impact of the debt-servicing charges are totally disastrous for the Atlantic provinces. Balance of payments considerations show the same trend, for balance of payments figures must be strongly positive to survive, given the need to service the debt structure, rather than be strongly negative, as is the case here. The Atlantic provinces simply could not survive in their present forms.

This is fully consistent with a 1991 study that noted, among other things, that federal transfers and expenditures in these provinces represented a full 33 percent of final domestic demand (1989 data), and that federal subsidies as a share of provincial budgetary revenue were in the 40 percent range.[58] The same study applies a computer simulation to the Newfoundland economy on the assumption that federal subsidies end. The results model population declines of up to 50 percent and income declines of up to 40 percent, though, if you are looking for any available good news, these are tradeoffs. In other words, you can maintain incomes fairly well through massive outmigration, or you can more or less maintain present population through a huge drop in income. But the overall picture is bleak. The overall Atlantic result would be similar.

The province-by-province measures of reduced GDP put the story in its most dramatic perspective. There is no doubt about it: the Atlantic on its own will not be "viable" by any definition without enormous change.

---

58 Douglas May and Dane Rowland in *From East to West: Regional views on Reconfederation*, C.D. Howe Institute, 1991.

Moving west, let us stop briefly in Quebec, even though this book assumes its decision to leave has already been taken. Though much better off than is the Atlantic, the new Quebec will have some worries of its own. The drop in GDP is serious, and of course this figure takes no account of any other problems introduced by separation. The debt-to-GDP ratios are well off the accepted international scale and point to potential trouble. Perhaps more worrisome is the balance of trade number, especially when it is recalled that this is a *pre-breakup* number, and will have to be adjusted both for trade disruption (and for exceptional new exports if possible) and also for the fact that not only will Quebec no longer be the recipient of about $3 billion in net federal cash every year, but it will also have to find a tremendous amount of foreign exchange to pay its foreign-denominated debt. And all of this comes when it already starts with a significant negative balance of trade.

This generally weak position is why Mr. Parizeau does not want to assume direct responsibility for Quebec's share of the federal debt, but wants to merely pay the interest to Ottawa in Canadian dollars, leaving the credit guarantee to the rest of us. There is no doubt the rest of Canada will wish Quebec well, but such good wishes are unlikely to extend to this sort of agreement.

Moving on to Ontario, this province will be in quite good shape. Its debt ratios are uncomfortable but manageable. Its standard of current consumption actually increases, and its balance of trade position is good. Indeed, when one adds the trade balance to the net funds no longer taken from Ontario by Ottawa for distribution across the country, the position is even better. Unmeasured here, of course, is the decline in Ontario's exports of goods and services to the rest of Canada which would certainly result under this scenario.

Saskatchewan/Manitoba will be in trouble. It will not be nearly as bad as will the Atlantic, but it will not be comfortable. The debt ratios are not good, nor is the balance of payments situation. The current consumption drop would be very painful, as we could imagine if, say, an increase in mortgage payments on our own houses suddenly forced us to cut consumption by such a percentage. It will indeed be looking for someone to associate with.

Both Alberta and British Columbia are fairly well off. Like Ontario, their current consumption doesn't change by much and the debt ratios are even better than that of the largest province. Alberta has a stronger balance of payments position than does B.C. In addition, for these two provinces (and indeed for every province), world exports would be boosted by a presumably weaker currency if that unit was still the Canadian dollar, in some way or other.[59]

The theoretical combination of Alberta and B.C. would, of course, be healthy, though both the Prairie and the "Canada West" groups would be a little stretched as to debt.

In short, regarding the economic viability question, the Atlantic will face a total transformation in population and income, unless some sort of major inter-regional subsidy package continues after a breakup. Saskatchewan/Manitoba will really need to look for a friend, and the rest will get by, before taking into account the immeasurable, but almost certainly high, transition and reorganization costs.

One other "region" should be mentioned, and that is Ottawa itself. In examining table 8.1, we note that every province except Ontario will be required to make important—sometimes disastrous—reductions in the old "federal-type" expenditures if the country breaks up. We may be very sure that the kinds of former Ottawa expenditures that the-off-on-their-own provinces will continue to make will be of the absolutely essential, local variety. They will not be able to afford to pay for the Ottawa establishment any more.

In practical terms, this means that essentially all of the foreign affairs, aid, and defence sections would be gone, except as Ontario might want to pay for their continuance for its own economic purposes, Ottawa residents being otherwise eligible for Ontario welfare. Newfoundland would find the funds to operate its lighthouses, but the Coast Guard headquarters in Ottawa would be gone. Saskatchewan might

---

59   If, however, all provinces were forced into joining the United States dollar club by the disappearing of the Canadian dollar, the effects would be different. The export ability of the weaker provinces would increase as real wages declined. The effect in Ontario, B.C., and Alberta might be in the other direction, i.e., capital inflows might actually weaken terms of trade.

continue local wheat research, but would have no money for Agriculture Canada employees in Ottawa. The national funding agencies for research and culture would be gone, with consequences reaching far beyond Ottawa. B.C. would run its fishery and ports, but Fisheries and Oceans Canada, and Ports Canada would be gone.

And what of Ottawa's other obligations in such a scenario? To the U.S. space project? Gone, and the U.S. can afford that. But how about obligations to retired public servants, even without considering retired Bloc Québécois MPs? The fragments of ROC just might pay the bond-holders of the old Canada to protect their own credit ratings, but the "junior creditors," as public service pensioners would be in such a scenario, might suffer the usual fate of unsecured debenture holders in a corporate reorganization, which is a loss of some or all of their income. The unfunded portion of the CPP would, of course, be out the window, except as any province might be able to pick it up, and that is also true of the OAP and other such payments to persons. If the provincial governments could handle it, these payments might continue, or they might be seriously cut back.

UI could be continued at some level in every province, but in the poorer provinces, it would be cut drastically, as it is in effect a transfer payment (see earlier chapters).

The politics of all this is obvious. It is *highly* in the interest of at least six of ten provinces to make *almost any* deal that preserves the Canadian support system in some form, even if the current standard can't be afforded. I refer to this in Chapter 10: "Plan C." It is also much in the interests of Ottawa residents and Ottawa dependents to support such a move. The tradeoff, however, is the end of the "Ottawa system" of government.

Political viability of different forms of government for ROC or its fragments

There is another form of viability that must be measured for any state, and that measure is *political*. Unless people can agree on a form of living together, the economics of the situation don't really matter, as many affluent professional couples have found in the divorce experience.

Therefore, this section looks at what forms of government might be available to ROC and its parts to make the politics work.

The case of an individual province configuration is quite simple. The federal level would disappear, the provincial governments would become "national" governments, and political life would go on, as long as the economy worked. The new states might want to make marginal internal changes in such areas as county or regional district powers, but this is just useful fiddling.

The case of the Atlantic would appear to be the next simplest, for there surely could be no thought of affording more than one govern-ment, given the economic consequences of forced independence. Alas, it may not be so simple.

We return to the reality of islands, which is as much a state of mind as it is a statement of geography. Newfoundland and Prince Edward Island are geographically distinct. There are no artificial lines around them, just a lot of water.

This is true of Newfoundland in particular. (One realizes that Labrador exists, on the mainland, but the politics and mindset are totally dominated by the island itself.) With a massive outmigration and a sufficiently revised power deal on Churchill Falls,[60] who knows what might be devised? And on the other side, Nova Scotia and New Bruns-wick are a long ways away, both in accessibility and mindset. Some will say that Newfoundland will be no worse off on its own once Canada is gone.

P.E.I. is much smaller, and is changing almost daily with the very powerful economic and emotional fact of the "fixed link" to the main-land, now under construction. It would probably throw its lot in with New Brunswick.

---

60   This is an extremely important matter, which feeds back into the economic viability of both Newfoundland and Quebec. An estimate published in 1991 in *Power Play: Bitter memories of a bad deal that may poison the future of hydro in Labrador* by Beth Gorham suggests that Quebec makes an annual profit of $800 million on that power. Newfoundland would no doubt ask ROC to seek ways to recapture some or all of that.

New Brunswick and Nova Scotia have a lot in common, but the bilingual, bicultural reality of Acadia is a difference. If this could be accommodated, the formation of a single Maritime nation looks likely. The concept of a multi-province Maritime federation could scarcely be supported. The Maritimes would be in a state of true emergency, and reality would require shrinking not only the population, but also the government, instead of paying a new bunch to replace those in Ottawa.

If there were any real mutual interest on both sides of the table (the Maritimes and Washington) for a union with the United States, whatever group of former provinces that was to join would clearly have to join as a single entity. The United States Senate is such a delicately-balanced and important organism that it would not dream of adding more than two new Senators from the Atlantic fragment of socialistic Canada!

It is complicated, and it is doleful to contemplate. No part of the former Canada would have more difficulty in accommodating not only its economics, but also its rich political history, to the new circumstances than would the Maritimes.

In this part of the survey we pass quickly over post-independence Quebec, because much work has been done on this already, and this book is really about ROC. And so moving westward, we arrive at Ontario. This giant-among-Canadians, if shorn of its empire, will be little more than a sort of Pennsylvania of the north—lots of people, lots of industry, a bit of access to the ocean, and huge markets in every direction. (However, unlike Pennsylvania, Ontario would not have the advantage of having two members in the U.S. Senate.)

The icing on the Ontario cake has always been its export of goods and services to the other provinces. It has done particularly well in the clean and lucrative areas of business and financial services. Of course, the other side of the equation has been its immense contributions back, through the recycling suction pump of Ottawa.

And Ontario is *big*. It is so big, in both population and size, that, if Queen's Park were to absorb the nation-state duties formerly carried out by Ottawa, it might feel comfortable devolving some of its own provincial powers to its own regions. If so, that might provide an opening for an arrangement with Saskatchewan and Manitoba, to the benefit of all sides.

If they could get together with Ontario, the prairie provinces would keep at least one wheat port, Thunder Bay, within their own new country, and Toronto would have a little bit of the old game left in terms of selling goods and services. It would be a small part of the old pie, it is true, but when times are tough you look for bits and pieces. And an Ontario freed of its current enormous transfers to the Atlantic[61] would easily be able to keep up subsidies to its old prairie friends. In this there could be the basis of a deal.

But the deal would have to be on the basis of a single, unitary state, not a federation. The numbers are too out-of-whack, since Saskatchewan and Manitoba *together* total only twenty percent of Ontario. Moreover—and this will be important further west as well—if the old federation has broken, the idea of federations will be tarnished for a time for former Canadians, notwithstanding the fact that federalism is one of the greatest inventions of political history.

That is why a devolution of power to regions by the Ontario government, as it accepts the old powers of Ottawa, is a key concept, here. The existence of active regional powers, even if short of a true federation, would make the new circumstances a lot more palatable for Saskatchewan and Manitoba.

And moving west again, the idea of Alberta alone is simple enough, but might not a union connection with Saskatchewan and Manitoba run west towards Edmonton rather than east towards Queen's Park? After all, the three provinces are all part of what we have called "the Prairies" or "the West," and they engage in large amounts of agricultural production on flat land. They share a large overlap in population sourcing from the great European inflows of the early part of the century, and they all

---

61   If ROC does fragment to the point of the Atlantic going it alone, there will be an early surge of generosity and emotion in the "have" provinces of Ontario, Alberta and B.C. to attempt to cushion the Atlantic with ongoing subsidy payments of some kind. As the hard realities set in, this generosity will be sorely tested, producing unpredictable results.

feel outside of the power structure of central Canada. But there are important differences.

The basis of the differences is wealth. Where the hard-scrabble farmers of Saskatchewan and Manitoba had to stick together, as the small manufacturers of Winnipeg did through family ties, there grew a collective and cooperative mentality that has resulted in the enduring presence of the NDP in these two provinces. Even the Liberals made some showing in a Manitoba that much closer to Ontario, just that much more of a mixed economy.

The agriculture of Alberta has included much more ranching. Ranchers are less collective; the newer breed of oilmen that has so shaped Alberta for the past almost fifty years is even less so. And Alberta has always had more Americans—some from oil, some for other reasons—but the resultant blend has been distinctly more individualistic, populist, competitive, and conservative than that of its two neighbours to the east.

Social Credit was the provincial manifestation of this for forty years; Reform is the recent federal proof. The thesis is not that the prairie provinces are as different as oil and water; it is just that they have chosen different political philosophies to regulate their common affairs.

A new, three-province, Prairie "country" would require an upfront agreement on wealth transfers from Alberta to the other two. This would not likely sit as easily with the politics of Alberta as it would with that of Ontario. Moreover, since Saskatchewan and Manitoba are much more similar in size to Alberta than they are to Ontario, there *would* be insistence on a federation, with its two levels of government, once again paying a new group to do the old Ottawa's work.

But it would be more a union of equals, and hence would be attractive to Saskatchewan/Manitoba in that sense. One suspects that the "federal" level problem might be finessed not by actually having an elected "federal" structure for the three provinces, but rather by looking after these things through the device of a much cheaper Council of Ministers. Since much of what Ottawa now does could easily be devolved to the three provincial governments, this might be workable. (In principle the Maritimes could follow the same route. The problem is the cost of maintaining the three *provincial* governments, a situation which the Prairies, more populous and richer, could handle.)

In the end, it is hard to say which way Saskatchewan/Manitoba would go—east or west. It would be a curious contest: more enthusiastic bidding from Ontario despite a more traditional association with, and closer geographical proximity to, the province of Alberta.[62]

Our next little theoretical country is B.C./Alberta. On paper, this looks very good. The economics work, not just in terms of government finance, but in terms of the private sector as well. Recalling our principle of diversification, the two provinces complement each other nicely: energy and wood, agriculture and fish, coal and hardrock mining, tourism, and lots of foreign interest. Both entities have decent balances of payments. Alberta needs B.C. for access to the sea; B.C. needs Alberta for . . . there's the rub. For what? Other than for feeding the port of Vancouver, which is justified on a straight commercial basis with no need for a political union.

The question is truly hard to answer. This fact is strange in a way, for Alberta is a wonderful province by anyone's standards. And the differences of wealth with the other Prairie provinces do not exist here. But again, there are differences. And again, they show up in politics.

On the (federal) surface, they are the same: overwhelming representation by the Reform Party of Canada. But this is a first, and the Reform Party is still finding itself. In particular, the parties in B.C. and Alberta are different. Alberta was the birthplace of Reform, and the ideological commitment goes deep. In B.C., at least for voters if not for party members, Reform was strictly a *vehicle* in October of 1993. It was a way to send a message to Ottawa and all of the establishment parties that the old game was over. It was a vote "against," whereas in Alberta there was at least a balancing positive emotion of "for."

The difference shows up more clearly at the provincial level, where there are no confusing national cross-currents. B.C. is above all populist, and is after that a mix of conservatism and socialism, with the former

---

62 We tend to forget the huge vacant area in the centre of Canada. It is 1,518 kilometres from Winnipeg to Toronto, and, with all due respect to Thunder Bay, there are not many people in between.

being dominant, the latter occasionally coming up the middle. B.C. has a strong and enduring collectivist streak. It is also a society very deeply changed and shaped by immigration trends, which has shown up in the economy and in population data, but not yet in political behaviour. This is because the huge influx of Asian newcomers take time to become citizens, and time after that to become involved in politics. But that will come. And when it does, B.C. will have another distinction *vis-à-vis* Alberta.

The school population of Vancouver contains more than fifty percent English as a Second Language (ESL) students. The population of Vancouver in the 1991 census was 22 percent Chinese, of whom the majority are relative newcomers to Canada, plus other large and growing groups of new Canadians. British Columbia is changing fast, and will change faster. At a guess, the left-right balance of politics is not much affected by this, but views on such "national" issues as bilingualism, aboriginals, immigration, "Canadian culture," welfare, and national unity will probably be rather different. This is natural, since the newcomers see these things with a "Man from Mars" perspective, and a lot of it is difficult to understand and find sensible for anyone but a long-time inmate.

The two provinces are so powerful as stand-alone entities that neither one will be prepared to swallow many concessions in terms of union. It is hard to imagine that either would want much of an influence by the politics of the other. One might square that circle again by convening something too small to call a Council of Ministers, but maybe a Premier's Conference. In a total fragmentation scenario, the two provinces would surely want to cooperate; it seems equally likely that they would want to rule their own roosts.

The final configuration to analyze, short of a total ROC, is the "Canada West" idea, from the Ontario boundary to the Pacific. Once again, all of the practical factors work: government budgets, assistance to Saskatchewan and Manitoba, balance of payments, and so on. Curiously, the politics work better too.

The inclusion of Saskatchewan and Manitoba would do something for British Columbia that Alberta alone could not. Part of this, of course, is due to plain land mass. To a Canadian, vast quantities of real estate is a familiar and valued concept. The economic diversification factor would be increased a bit, but the two most important points lie in the realms of the emotional and the political.

On the emotional side, there will be a lot of regret about Canada breaking up, leading to a sense of abandoning cousins who are needy. Retaining a union with Saskatchewan and Manitoba helps assuage this sentiment, in spades. The West would be left with over half of Canada, not to be sneezed at, one-quarter of the population, and considerably more than its pro rata share of wealth.

On the political side, the left in British Columbia, understandably skittish about joining with Alberta on its own, could take comfort in the political views of Saskatchewan and Manitoba, as being rather more like those of B.C.

It would still be a bit hard to envision this four-province construct agreeing with the machinery of a new "federal government." (Indeed, one wonders if all of Canada together would invent such a device today!) But again, the Council of Ministers approach, perhaps with an advisory committee drawn from the four legislatures so as to include all political faiths, might work, as long as the "central" government were restricted to minimal functions.

And now the big question: what if ROC as a whole had a desire to stick together after Quebec was gone? What kind of machinery could conceivably make that work?

Most of us, not having thought about this at all, assume that business would continue as usual. Our whole federal system would carry on, absent Quebec, and downsized about one-quarter as the new population would warrant. Our current government might carry on, or we might have a new election, but the game would be the same.

Well, maybe. We have examined inertia. It is a very powerful force. And we are lawful people, us Canadians. All the laws of the land would be in place, *mutatis mutandis*, as the lawyers say, and we would just carry on. Our negotiators would do the deal with Quebec, the debt would be fairly split, access to the Atlantic region would be guaranteed, and we might still be eligible for the G-7 club. This is entirely logical—until you think about it. And then the answer becomes . . . .

Well, maybe not. Maybe someone, somewhere, blows a whistle that counts. Maybe someone says, "We don't like the way the old show worked, and we like the look of the new one even less. We want a new deal."

In my opinion, the forces referred to in Chapter 6 will sooner or later require major changes in ROC, or further separation. What one cannot foresee as of today is the trigger—the jiggle that unsticks inertia. But one thing is certain: it can only come from one of two places, British Columbia or Alberta.

The reason is simple. Everyone else is set upon a sea of woe if the long-running Canada party is called to an end. Alberta and British Columbia, in due course, do just fine. And the old rules don't really suit, so now that the issue has been opened up, why not insist on change? These voices will certainly be heard. The only issues are how loud they will be, how numerous their troops will be.

If those voices force no immediate reckoning, ROC will lumber on, until some combination of politics and finance stops it. That is one scenario. It is highly unlikely.

The likely scenario calls for a genuine discussion among the elements of ROC, to decide what to do. The ways and means of that dialogue is the subject of the next section. But for now, what new structure for ROC might have the best chance of success and longevity?

One can make some fairly certain observations, as follows:

1. The structure would have to be *federal*. There is no way so many diverse elements could be hived into a unitary state.

2. The ensuing federal government would probably be pretty loose, and restricted in its objectives. The poorer provinces would want it to do more, but they will not call the tune at a time like this. The richer provinces will want it to do less.

3. The control mechanism of this federal government might or might not be a Parliament. Our recent Parliaments have not earned a good name. There are two ways to go here, and this is very important.

If the elements of ROC have a sense that they have something to *accomplish* together—a set of shared goals that give meaning to common effort, and a reason to submerge local interests in pursuit of those greater goals—then ROC would want a Parliament, or some central elected body.

If, on the other hand, the federation is a matter of convenience, or of mutual advantage, and is really a service organization (which is not to be despised), then a real Parliament would only be troublesome, and one would want a Council of Ministers delegated by the provinces, advised by an advisory group of legislators drawn from the provincial Houses, at most.

(The European Union may have made a mistake in this regard. They have an important sounding board called the European Parliament, having high expectations and low powers. The European Union is in fact a service organization for its national states, and a true Parliament is not consistent with such limited objectives.)

4. The powers of the central government of ROC, if based on *de novo* agreement rather than inheritance from Canada, would surely be minor compared to those of the present. Indeed, the briefly famous "Allaire Report" of the Quebec Liberal Party might seem to be extravagant and generous to the central authority.[63]

When you think about it, the truly essential functions of a *central* government or service organization are few. They include:

- Security and Defence
- Customs and Immigration (already a joint responsibility with the provinces)
- Integrity of credit rating of inherited debt (and therefore new credit access)
- Currency (optional—someone else's can be used)

---

63   *A Quebec Free to Choose*, the report of the constitutional committee of the Quebec Liberal Party to the 25th Convention, January 28, 1991. Exclusive central authority was to be restricted to Defence, currency and "the common debt," customs and tariffs, and equalization. There was to be shared authority over native affairs, justice, taxation and revenue, fisheries, post office and telecommunications, immigration, foreign policy, transport, and financial institutions. A much longer list of other government authorities was to be exclusively Quebec's.

- External relations
- Enforcement of inter-regional agreements and rules, common market, et cetera
- Inter-regional income transfers, as agreed by the parties
- Weights, measures, and other such standards
- Necessary legal, tax, and administrative machinery to accomplish the above.

That is it. There is nothing more that is really *necessary*. I think something more could be justified, but perhaps not as a part of ROC. As a part of "Plan C," which might prevent the breakup of Canada and keep Quebec aboard, the central authority might do a few more things, and these are discussed in the last chapter. But in terms of reaching an agreement on a new government of ROC, functions beyond the above meagre measures might not pass muster in British Columbia and Alberta, and maybe in some other provinces.

Why not? This is why not: once you've been burdened with huge problems in some part of your life, like the failure of your federation, your mindset is clear, and it is this: let me avoid those problems henceforth!

And what apparently has caused the problems? The prime suspect will be federalism as we have practised it, the whole system, run by others for their benefit. (Every part of Canada might subscribe to this statement, which is a testament to the failure of governments.)

What else would rankle from the past? The list is long: entanglements with others who want different things, done different ways; government that is too big, and too far away; trust in that government, when we should not have done so; tolerance of financial excess and political games, when we should not have had it; dependency, when we should have stood on our own feet, this last from the Atlantic.

In short, people will have been badly burned. They will consider new arrangements first and foremost from the perspective of not being burned again, and that sentiment does not lead to an attitude of giving powers to others. It leads to wanting power close to home.

So as we leave this part, the landscape is not cheery. Indeed, what has been too little emphasized are the difficulties *everyone* would face.

To illustrate, look at the *most fortunate* of the provinces under this scenario, British Columbia. Look at the individual person.

Most people's wealth, if they have any, is in their homes. Suppose ROC is breaking up, but you are living in B.C. and you want to sell your home. This is the province of the future, Pacific Rim, Asian buyers, and so on. So there should be no problem, right? Not so. During the period of uncertainty as to what Quebec and ROC will do and what the former Canada will look like, you may be certain of three things:

- Foreigners will become worried about our debt, and will raise interest rates. This will make housing transactions harder to finance.
- The Canadian dollar will decline, making Canadian real estate "cheaper"—but where will the bottom of this decline be? Will it be even cheaper next month or next year? This hurts too.
- Potential Canadian buyers will be paranoid about their jobs and other investments, and won't feel like entering into any new transactions.

The above factors kill a real estate market, even one as buoyant as B.C.'s, the best in the country. What about all other Canadians? Don't try to sell your house.[64]

Talking to each other

The foregoing options for ROC are very disturbing. For most Canadians, this is a lose-lose situation—lose Quebec, and lose your standard of living. Only three provinces have much potential for coming out ahead,

---

64   As an interesting footnote, Ontario, B.C., and Alberta people—living in positive balance of payments provinces—may have an escape valve. They will be able to list and sell houses in United States dollars, with the much lower interest rates that go with that. U.S. banks would not be likely to step into a market they don't know with mortgage funds, but the Canadian banks have all of the U.S. dollar access required to make a decent mortgage market in U.S. dollars—as long as it is in an economically viable province.

This is a special case of the general observation whereby the U.S. dollar often becomes the de facto transaction vehicle in national states under pressure with an unreliable currency.

and only after a period of traumatic uncertainty that that will be painful even for them.

That said, once Quebec is gone, the world is going to change. There is just no doubt about that; it is simply a matter of time. It is in everyone's interests to take the time to carefully discuss the options, but it is in no one's interest to allow any delay beyond that. Uncertainty is extremely costly when it relates to the basics of national life. Wheels spin, energy is wasted, nothing happens, and matters get worse. Time is no friend here.

So ROC must talk. Indeed, the informal talk should start now. This taboo subject has to be aired and ventilated so thoroughly across the land that we are able to build a basic understanding of the choices. This understanding will serve us well if the need arrives, and the stark nature of the choices may give us the necessary wisdom and motivation to avoid them altogether. We must talk.

If and when the Parti Québécois wins an election, the dam of silence will break on this issue. Then, as part of our informal dialogue and education during the pre-referendum period, we will have time to consider the *formal* means of talking together after the referendum, if need be.

There are two basic ways to go in structuring these talks. One way involves governments; the other is a Constituent Assembly approach of people chosen by the voters for this sole purpose: to redesign our governments and boundaries if need be, subject to ratification by referendum in each province. Let us look at these methods in turn.

The first amounts to the familiar First Ministers' Conference, except that Ottawa might or might not be there. This would not really be relevant at that point. Unlike the normal conference, however, this one would be of huge importance, and decisions would have to be reached, even if it stretched over months.

More than this, the decisions reached would have to be enforceable, in the sense of gaining acceptance by the various provincial electorates, even if grudgingly. We earlier canvassed whether this might be achieved by simple First Ministerial agreement, without a popular (referendum) ratification process. In theory, this might still be done. In practice, would provincial governments take the risk?

With Quebec gone, the game is no longer to save Canada. The game is to save whatever you can, and one of the entities each premier will be looking to save is his or her own government. That requires paying a lot of attention to what the voters think in this most important of tasks. Any government that sets out for independence, or agrees to somehow reconstitute ROC, or anything in between, will want to know it has the support of at least a majority of its voters.

The only way to be demonstrably responsive to this need is to submit to a referendum whatever deal is made. The concept of referenda in constitutional matters is now so embedded in the Canadian political consciousness that it is very unlikely that provincial governments would proceed without this stamp of approval. And, of course, if even *one* province went that route, the others would be under huge pressure to do so as well. The bottom line is that whatever the new ROC or its pieces may look like, there will almost certainly be a referendum for ratification, throughout whatever grouping we are talking about, in all of ROC, if that is the deal that is made, or in the various new countries that are spawned by the process.

In other words, any deal must be *referendum-proof.*

Now, this is a problem. Most Canadians in most provinces neither particularly like nor trust their governments. Governments are something we must have, and can't be avoided, so we regularly troop to the polls, trying to choose the lesser of evils, and hoping it won't turn out to be the evil of lessers. The level of trust or acceptance is sufficient to get us through the regular routine of budgets and laws, but if we arrive at something as important as the shape of a country, a confidence gap opens up.

In ordinary governmental matters, this makes no difference. The laws are passed, and that is that. Throw the rascals out at the next election if you like, but that's all you can do.

If there is to be a referendum on the matter at hand, that is very different. Constitutional questions are intrinsically complicated. Most people have to go on trust. If trust is lacking, the tendency is to vote "No." Yet, obviously, if we get many "No" votes in the process of restructuring a country, we have a problem.

Moreover, as pointed out before, not one government in this country (with the possible exception of the Parti Québécois) will have been
elected on constitutional issues, or for its constitutional expertise. Not
even remotely so! The result is that the voters will have no prior
knowledge nor expectations of the constitutional positions those governments might adopt on their behalf if they go to a bargaining table.
Such a process might succeed, but that would be quite a surprise.

(It would also be an unreasonable expectation. These folks have not
even been able to agree on removing barriers to interprovincial trade,
nor on setting common educational standards for reference.)

A Constituent Assembly

Fortunately, there is another way, which is also better. This would
involve the mechanism of a modified Constituent Assembly. This device would solve the problem of trust, being specifically elected to
perform this task (of developing a restructuring plan), and no other. It
would also solve the problem of expertise, through the election process,
and other means to be described below.

The idea of constituent assemblies crafting constitutions is neither
new nor untried. The constitutions of the United States (1787), Australia
(1898), West Germany (1948), and Spain (1978) were all drawn up by
assemblies. All did their work promptly. Spain took by far the longest,
at eight months. The recent South African miracle was done in a similar
fashion, with due allowance for the fact that representative delegates
could not be chosen by election.

The idea is perfectly applicable to Canada, and I have outlined in
detail the specifics as they might have worked, pre-Charlottetown
Accord, in a previous paper.[65] Some modification to the details of
previous plans would have to be made today, to accommodate the
curious circumstances of ROC.

The new element here is that provincial delegates to the Assembly
would meet those of other provinces on a rather conditional basis, rather

---

65   "What if the Wheels Fall Off the Constitutional Bus?" Canada West
Foundation, May 1992.

than on the simpler "How do we save Canada?" basis that would have been the case prior to the difficulties caused by the Accord. The goal would not be so clear because the positions of others on crucial issues would no longer be clear. For example, the goal for the Alberta delega- tion might or might not be for a "ROC preserved." It might turn out to be for Canada West, Alberta-B.C., or something else.

Therefore, there would be a much greater degree of provincial caucusing and consultation of provincial advantage, rather than there being the pan-Canadian view that the non-Quebec delegates might have taken in an earlier, simpler time. This is by no means bad. A deeper acquaintance with reality is a good thing, and the pan-Canadian senti- ment of recent years outside of Quebec has concealed some important and growing strains that have to be addressed.

But apart from that, the basic idea of a Constituent Assembly to discuss constitutional issues remains in force. To briefly recap my 1992 work, the essence is as follows:

Purpose

The job of the Assembly will be to hammer out a new form of govern- ment to meet the new circumstances, on behalf of the people it repre- sents. The proposals will then be put to those people in a referendum for ratification (or not).

(There are undefined words in this statement, which must be clari- fied, and will be. "The people it represents" could end up being all of ROC, or just individual provinces, voting one province at a time, for example.)

Requirements it must meet

These include:
- Legality
- Legitimacy
- Representativeness
- Vision
- Plenary Authority
- Timeliness

A brief word on each follows, bearing in mind that whatever this group comes up with must command sufficient respect to win a referendum vote.

Regarding *legality*, nothing will be simple. If Canada goes, what will be left of the authority of Parliament, the Supreme Court, and so on? Nevertheless, we are not a revolutionary people. A Constituent Assembly, in order to do its work well, will need the blessings of governments. The blessing of every participating province is essential (and some may not participate, which is not fatal). This is because the provinces will be the functioning governments—the ones that people will pay attention to—after the loss of Quebec.

The blessing of Ottawa will be an added advantage. It is, however, not essential, in the same way that the blessing of a football coach is mostly irrelevant in light of talks as to whether or not his team is going to stay together. (The irrelevance of Ottawa in these difficult times will be entirely suitable. It has for some years been more part of the problem than the solution. The current Ottawa government has dealt with this by denying any problem exists.)

It is important to think about this pitiable giant of Ottawa in these circumstances, for many—probably most—Canadians still think that the direction and answers will come from that place. That will not be the case. To repeat an earlier observation: if Ottawa fails in its most basic, fundamental, and important duty of national unity, evidenced by the departure of Quebec, why pay this extraordinarily costly and arrogant head office any further heed, or money? This feeling will not take long to sink in for the "have" provinces. The others will want to continue the old game, but it will be over.

So in short, the first legality of new arrangements will come from the blessing of a Constituent Assembly by (participating) provincial governments. The ultimate legality, of course, can only come from the electorate in a referendum. And after that, *formal* legality will have to come from the affirmative acts of Legislatures, in order to avoid a dangerous legal discontinuity.

As to *legitimacy*, we must feel that our people at the Assembly absolutely represent us. These representatives will have to make some very tough judgement calls and tradeoffs. They can consult during the process, but these things are complex, and the details will be left to their judgements. The electorate will only accept this kind of responsibility from people mandated to do that job. That is why a special election to choose these single-purpose representatives will be required.

On *representativeness*, this is the greatest and most important challenge, for it is crucial to the "legitimacy" point, and will not automatically come out of elections. Indeed, it would be surprising if we chose any others than the very best we could find for this purpose, and therefore, almost by definition, this would not be a collection of "ordinary people." Fortunately, a more global representativeness can be achieved by having a mix of "talking" and "voting" participants in the Assembly, as described in the membership section.

Vision is more a prayer than a job description, more a hope than a requirement. We must look beyond the problems of the day to the opportunities of the future. To secure such paladins we can only rely on the voters.

Plenary authority means simply that the Assembly is in charge of its own work. It might be attractive to some to say in advance, "Keep ROC together," or, "Do not touch the Charter," or, "At all costs retain a Parliamentary system." That would be unwise. The real bedrock of our lives will not be at risk from such a group. Designating untouchable principles would be controversial in itself, and such a list would be potentially endless. And a "Keep the ROC" pre-condition would abort the exercise at once.

Timeliness means simply that the Assembly must get about its business. The experience in other lands indicates that this is not a problem as long as incentives run the right way. For ROC, the timing will be "with all deliberate speed," for many lives will be on hold during the process. And most importantly, timeliness will determine how the recommendations of the Assembly will be handled once delivered. It must be quickly. The three year framework of Meech Lake will be out of the question for a country in a breakup mode. Ratification votes must be virtually immediate.

Membership

Remembering that the first duty of a Constituent Assembly is to produce a plan that has a good chance of being accepted by the folks back home, it is clear that one will want a membership of whom most people would say, "O.K.—if that group is for it, I guess I am too."

Exactly the reverse applied in the attempted marketing of the Charlottetown Accord. The personalities of the sponsors, namely, the First Ministers, led many to automatically vote against whatever that group was for. This will continue to be the case for any major constitutional revision presented by First Ministers. They carry too much baggage, and have too many enemies from totally unrelated wars.

The members of the Constituent Assembly should be selected for that Assembly purpose, and that purpose only. They should do their jobs, and go home.

Clearly, the key players must be elected. If we choose delegates, we will presumably have more confidence in them than we would if they were chosen by someone else. Each participating province should elect a delegation of perhaps ten persons, who would caucus and vote as a province.[66] This is a reflection of what will be the reality: provincial boundaries are pro-tem the only ones that count. I will call these elected persons "voting delegates."

Imagine the members of the "dream team" for your province at this Assembly. Most of those people would be available for the job, if it were guaranteed they could go home and mind their business after that. We would end up with the best of our politicians, but only a few of them. In an election to such an Assembly, people would have no truck with political parties. Individual offerings would be the key, and some, or even many, of those elected would not be practicing politicians at all.

Election will produce a respected Assembly. However, as noted above, it will not necessarily produce a representative or well-informed Assembly, and these things are essential, of course. Therefore, representatives and expertise must be supplied by other means. It will be entirely appropriate for defined groups within our society to have representa-

---

66   See decision making rules, below.

tive delegates. First among these are governments. Governments are the repository of much constitutional, legal. and economic expertise which should be fully utilized. Each participating government (including the residual Ottawa) should have the right to appoint, say, two delegates.

Other recognized groups within our society—what one might call "identifiable collectives"—should also have the right of delegate appointment, to make sure that major interest groups and minorities have a guaranteed voice. After all, if they are not able to be heard inside the Assembly, they will find the process less than legitimate, and the process must above all be positive and unifying rather than divisive. The appropriate list of groups will depend on the forces of the day, but, in my opinion, it should be generously drawn.

It would be wise to include in this group a representative set of legislators from each province, chosen by the Legislature. Politicians will have to be part of the solution. Legislatures will have to implement any agreements, so politicians should be a part of getting there.

Finally as to membership, the Assembly itself might want to appoint a few "experts" in constitutional matters, for all of this has been done before somewhere in the world, and the Assembly should know about those cases.

All of these *appointed* delegates, from governments and groups, I will call "talking delegates."

Decision rules

The two important questions are *who will vote*, and *how will the votes be counted*?

Recalling the structuring of the membership, the "voting delegates" must be those, and only those, who are elected for the purpose.

Every delegate will get to talk, to lobby, to present positions and arguments. Then the voting delegates will decide. The simple analogy is the courtroom. The judge and the lawyers get to give advice. It is the jury that decides. People understand and have trust in this approach— the ancient concept of a "jury of one's peers."

Counting the votes is a bit more complicated, and requires a brief return to the first principles as to why this Assembly will have been established.

Our assumption for this point in time is that Quebec will have made its decision to go, and that specialized negotiators will be at work on that issue. The rest of us will have to decide what *we* want to do. Talking that out will be the job of the Assembly.

To achieve proper participation, clearly there can be no preconditions, and it must be called with the assent of the participating provinces. If, for example, Ottawa attempted to call a Constituent Assembly whose precondition was the formalization of ROC with no other options to be considered, some provinces might not come, particularly Alberta and B.C. who have perhaps had enough of being outvoted by central Canada. Or, they might come in a mood to force a change in the maintenance-of-ROC precondition, which would quickly dissipate the necessary positive climate.

But this has implications, of course. If provinces have choices—if they are true plenary players here—then at least one voting rule is simple: agreement on the final product must be unanimous among the provinces.[67]

Here are four comments on the entirely sensible observation that unanimity is very difficult in this world. The first is this: the Fathers of Confederation did it in 1867. So did the 13 American States in 1787.

The second comment helps to explain why they were successful. It is that the penalty for rejecting the final product is that the nay-saying province simply will not be a part of the deal. That will be such an enormous penalty (for every province except Alberta and B.C.) that the likelihood would be extremely high that at least everyone else would get together. (One recalls that P.E.I. was not prepared to accept the 1867 deal, and only came in a few years later. The world did not end. A couple of the 13 American states opposed the negotiated package, but finally backed down and came aboard, after minor changes.)

The third comment is that all votes *prior* to finalization could be cast on a looser voting schedule, a variant of which is presented below.

---

67   This does *not* mean unanimity among the *delegates*. Provincial votes would be determined by a majority of the provincial delegates, perhaps with the provincial government representative casting a vote in the case of a tie.

The fourth comment is that there really is no alternative to unanimity. In the world of post-Quebec independence, provinces will be in a position to do things only by agreement, not by coercion, in restructuring their affairs. This reality has to be recognized. The need for unanimity of all those who want to be part of any continuing entity is a fact, not a theory or a whim.

On the many intermediate decisions leading up to the final package, some sort of weighted voting might be devised, perhaps one that works on a variant of the "seven and fifty" rule in our current constitution, revised as will be necessary in the absence of Quebec. This might assist in the step-by-step building of a provisional document, with the final, tough tradeoffs being done at the end.

Nuts and bolts

There will be a considerable amount of additional technical and administrative detail involved in setting up a Constituent Assembly, none of which involves reinventing the wheel. For many of these details, readers are referred to the Canada West publication cited above.

Ratification

As suggested above, once (and if) a deal were made, the appropriate ratification procedure would be to hold a referendum in each province. Given the process, if the Assembly could make a deal, there is a high probability that it would be accepted by the people. Failing that, governments would have to take the chance of imposing a new constitution, or risk returning to the drawing board. There are no other alternatives, and this one will give us our best shot.

Concluding observations

This process might or might not produce a deal to continue ROC. It might instead produce two or more new and smaller countries, drawn from the menu cited above. That will be part of the post-Quebec reality.

The next and very important point is this: if it *did* produce an ongoing form of government for ROC, it would almost certainly be a vastly pruned back central authority, amounting to little more than a vehicle for international continuity and a service bureau for the provinces. For reasons previously elaborated, it would be quite surprising if any more than this could be agreed upon. That might still be better than the alternative.

The third point regards timing. In principle, there is no reason why a Constituent Assembly could not be called right now to pre-empt the terrible dislocation we will all go through by virtue of the mere election of a separatist government of Quebec, even before a referendum takes place. There is absolutely no sign that Ottawa would be prepared to take that kind of risk, i.e., the risk of a Constituent Assembly producing a draft constitution drastically cutting back the role of Ottawa in exchange for continuity in the country. This would totally deflate the separatists if it were to happen, but the current Ottawa approach makes it unlikely. This is too bad.

The final point is this: even if something like a Constituent Assembly were not called until *after* Quebec has voted to go, it would still be highly intelligent to include Quebec observers as a part of the process. One should never give up. And as we shall see, they might want to be a part of Plan "C."

Chapter 9: Reprise and Stock-taking

IT WILL BE USEFUL AT THIS POINT to survey the rather cheerless path of future history we have travelled in this book so far.

Chapter 1 set out the reasons why we might want to think about what will happen if the existing Canada were broken up by the departure of Quebec. One of these is damage control, and there can be no doubt, after any inquiry of this kind, that there will be a lot of damage to control. It says:

1. There is a possibility that Quebec will vote to separate, and thus start a process that will dramatically change Canada as we know it. The possibility may be small—we don't know that—but it is certainly not zero.

2. The consequences and dangers, if this process begins, are so important that we must examine them in advance and have a contingency plan. Moreover, since this plan will of necessity involve all Canadians, all of us must talk about it.

3. Common sense, and the experience of other countries, tells us that the odds of Canada breaking up will be considerably increased by the election of a separatist government.

4. Thinking about "the unthinkable" in advance can be very useful to avoid or lessen the problem. Refusing to do advance thinking can lead to serious mistakes.

5. Conceivably, some good could come of our current tensions, if we handle them intelligently.

Chapter 2 models the period from the election of an assumed separatist Parti Québécois government in Quebec later on this year—probably in September or October of 1994—up until a referendum held by that government. It suggests that:

6. The election of a PQ government will immediately create major uncertainty, in Canada, and for our international lenders and customers. Uncertainty is always costly.

7. The PQ has promised an early referendum on independence, but the timing will not be wholly in its control. It will wait for the most promising time, which could considerably extend the period of uncertainty.

8. During the pre-referendum period, the federal government will be totally preoccupied with Quebec. Provincial governments and individuals in ROC will have to think about their own affairs.

9. ROC and Ottawa are not the same thing at all. Ottawa has an interest in maintaining its own position, which is not necessarily what ROC will need.

10. The tactical questions on both sides are complex, and the negotiations will be rough. These tactics will have an important continuing impact on relations *after* the referendum, for good or for ill.

11. Immediately following the unity debate in importance, international debt management will be the most dangerous single issue during this period.

12. Solutions are described that Ottawa could use to forestall or channel the separatist mood at this point. They will almost certainly not be adopted.

13. Instead, both sides will likely go the confrontation, dice-rolling route.

14. Possibilities of violence will exist during this period. Authorities on both sides of the Ottawa River must keep the peace vigorously, even if it means suppressing their own supporters.

15. The referendum margin is likely to be thin, one way or the other. This will have adverse consequences either way.

Chapter 3 and the balance of the book are predicated on the assumption that "the unthinkable" happens: that Quebeckers give majority support to an independence referendum. This chapter deals with the elements of the necessary transition to the new reality. If a referendum passes, then:

16. Immediate, strong, believable, and unconditional reassurances to foreign capital by all relevant authorities must be given at once, to avoid very painful effects on our standard of living. Indeed, these assurances should already be generally expected as a result of previous statements, which will be confirmed after the referendum.

17. An agreement to continue all laws and practices in force for a given period to prepare to talk—is very much in the interests of all parties.

18. There will be immediate crises of legitimacy in Ottawa, and in ROC. Until this is sorted out, useful responses to the new situation will be impossible.

19. The Ottawa position may be to carry on as if it were still in charge (which would not work), or to call an election, or to call a referendum. Whichever action is taken, the role of the provinces in what is to come will become pre-eminent.

20. A legitimate negotiating committee will have to be struck, to bargain with Quebec. (The alternative of refusing to negotiate is canvassed in Appendix I.)

21. The constitutional validation of any negotiated settlement will be a tricky question.

22. The far more important issue for most of us will not be Quebec. It will be the future of ROC, which receives almost no attention because the focus is on Quebec.

23. The glue holding the rest of Canada together may fail at this point.

Chapter 4 begins the analysis of the common and disparate interests of the components of ROC, in policy, economic, and political terms. Most of the few writers on this issue have simply assumed that the rest of Canada would go on together, much as before. This book says that is only one of the possibilities, and not necessarily the most likely one.

24. The "standard" assumption of a united ROC presupposes a sort of glue that will stand up under the new strains. A geographical and numerical description of such an entity shows what those strains might be.

25. The political structure of ROC will certainly have to change dramatically, and many of the economic and policy tradeoffs that have been made over the years will lose their stability, either because of the departure of Quebec, or as a consequence of a back-to-the-basics re-examination.

26. The current regional distribution of federal funds is set out, and is considered unsustainable, as "losers" and "winners" are identified in stark terms.

27. Money is not the only question. There are also "losers" and "winners" in the application of federal policies on culture, immigration, trade policy, and other such matters which will heighten the strains.

28. The political ideologies of the regions have some significant differences.

29. The conclusion is that the ROC could very well split, post-Quebec.

In many ways, **Chapter 5** is the most important one in the book. Its message is that the attitudes with which we approach this challenge—not only our attitudes on Quebec, but even more importantly on the continuity of ROC—will determine whether we see maximum or minimum damage, or even a win for everyone. The main points are:

30. The attitude of the rest of the world, especially in the United States, will be one of correct and benign non-interference. If the country does break up, the rest of the world will seek any advantage it can find in the new circumstances. ROC should not expect any favours.

31. The attitude of Quebec post-referendum will be cooperative and rational in almost any circumstance short of an attack on territorial integrity. Reality will require such an attitude: Quebec will need help.

32. The people of ROC must decide whether to be emotional or rational. In the opinion of this book, we must get through and past our emotions, and deal with the new situation on a strictly rational basis. We should make decisions strictly related to our interests and those of our grandchildren, and not out of any motives of anger or punishment, for that will harm our grandchildren.

33. Moral questions as to the preservation of the rights of minorities and "No!" voters within Quebec will arise. These should be dealt with through our negotiators to obtain adequate guarantees with respect to the legal, property, and government service rights of such minorities.

34. Native and anglophone minorities will have very significant bargaining clout of their own to add to this process, and it will be much in the interests of Quebec to accommodate them.

35. The issue of boundaries is the large potential flash point. We should attempt to secure minority protection through negotiation and guarantees rather than through boundary amendments. Any intervention to enforce guarantees not honoured should only take place under United Nations rules.

36. Some violence will be likely, in any case. It can only be contained within reasonable limits if both the governments concerned and the general public believe and enforce the rule that the use of violence, official or otherwise, is not appropriate between old and civilized friends, even as they draw apart.

37. What we are really talking about here is a restructuring of governments. As long as all the citizens concerned are dealt with fairly, a democratically-approved proposal to restructure governments is not worth waging a war over—except, perhaps, to the governments concerned.

Chapter 6 outlines the internal options for ROC, in order to fully present the array of factors to be considered in the following two chapters. (These describe how we might talk with Quebec about our relationship with it, and discuss with each other in ROC the relationship among ourselves.) The more important points here include:

38. The character of western alienation is in a process of change, moving away from "wanting in" on the Ottawa system, towards rejecting it (Ottawa, that is, not Canada). This will cause a real examining of that "Ottawa system" if Quebec leaves.

39. Whether or not ROC stays in one piece, it is clear that major changes in political structure will be required.

40. Many of the current duties of Ottawa could easily be absorbed by the provinces. New machinery would be required for a few "nation-state" duties if the Ottawa system were discarded.

41. If ROC subdivides, the probable new units would be the Atlantic, Ontario, B.C., and Alberta. Saskatchewan/Manitoba would have to make an alliance with either its eastern or western neighbour.

42. ROC as a whole and all of its components are fairly significant on a world scale. There are wide variations in debt load.

43. There are massive net federal transfers of funds to the Atlantic and Saskatchewan/Manitoba under the existing system. Quebec is only a small net beneficiary before taking the annual federal deficit into consideration, and a large loser, like the rest of the provinces, after taking this into account.

44. The huge burden of debt will precipitate a painful financial restructuring of our federal system whether there is a unity crisis or not.

Chapter 7 talks about bargaining with Quebec. It maintains that:

45. Our bargaining must be based on a rational approach to our interests, even though that approach will be exactly what the separatists want.

46. We will have a very considerable number of bargaining levers, which we should use with calculation, to our maximum benefit.

47. The negotiations must have the benefit of an informed public, even if this limits bargaining flexibility.

48. Ottawa will be so deeply mired in conflict with respect to the negotiations (possibly for reasons of personality, but more deeply because an agreement with Quebec will lead to a much down-sized Ottawa under *any* scenario) that the provinces will have to control the negotiations, possibly in concert with a new federal Parliament elected for that purpose.

49. Extended paralysis is a distinct possibility. This will have major costs.

50. Quebec boundaries will be a flash point. We should not try to change them.

51. Perpetual "innocent passage" access, without any tariff or fee, to the Atlantic via the South Shore will be obtained.

52. The currency issue will give some leverage to ROC, though it will not be definitive.

53. Responsibility for the existing federal debt will be the central question. It should be settled on population ratios, with minor adjustments. It will be better for everyone to obtain a rapid solution to this. Indeed, there are arguments for doing so *now*.

54. When all is said and done, the Quebec negotiations will be a sideshow for ROC, though this has captured almost all of our attention up to now. The truly important issue is how we will structure our own (ROC) affairs in the post-referendum world.

We come to the heart of the book in **Chapter 8.** Here we examine the elements of a "Plan B": how ROC might live together, or apart, after Quebec is gone. The major conclusions are:

55. The departure of Quebec will end the delicate balance that has sustained the Canadian trade-offs. The same balances will no longer work for ROC.

56. Two provinces, Alberta and British Columbia, have both the reasons and the muscle to force a total reappraisal of the old deal. The political inclination to move in this direction is growing.

57. The model for Quebec separation can easily serve as a model for the partition of ROC.

58. The principles of the design of political units give no clear support for the continuation of ROC, from the point of view of the wealthier provinces.

59. In a disassembled ROC, the Atlantic will do terribly, Ontario will survive, and the West will do well. Of all of the potential fragments, "Canada West" would probably work best, but it is unclear whether the grouping would be attractive enough for B.C. to take part.

60. ROC as a whole would work, but probably only on the basis of the vestigial central "government" being no more than a service organization for the highly autonomous provinces. This would be the bottom line of the richer provinces, which would call the shots (or not take part).

61. Examined in this context, the problem of the current Canada is not Quebec at all. The problem is "Ottawa" as a symbol of our brand of federalism.

62. ROC will have to talk to decide what to do. This might be done by First Ministers, though a Constituent Assembly would be more likely to produce acceptable results.

63. A Constituent Assembly could proceed according to well known rules, proven in many other countries. This is neither a novel nor an adventuresome concept, except insofar as it would almost certainly dispense with the current Ottawa system.

64. The end result is uncertain. But one thing is clear: whether as a single ROC or a multiplicity of new countries, most inhabitants of ROC (possibly not all) would be worse off than we are today. And Ottawa would be the biggest loser of all.

This summary of results is certainly not very pleasant. Put briefly, all Canadians today may expect to go through a turbulent and costly transition period that will disrupt their lives. With luck, we will then achieve a new status whose major achievement is getting rid of the Ottawa system that caused the debt and political problem in the first place—but it will be too late!

Some variation of the above is "Plan B." It is surely better to have a "Plan B" than it is to have no plan at all. There is simply no doubt about that. If nothing else, a Plan B will very markedly reduce the horrible transition costs and will limit the time of uncertainty. But it will be no fun. Happily, there is a better way, though the chances of success are slim.

Chapter 10:
"Plan C"

IF CHAPTER 8 WAS THE HEART OF THIS BOOK, this final one is the soul. Because there is a better way.

The stock-taking of the last chapter reveals a situation in which just about every part of Canada is poorer, at least in a material way, than is the situation today. And indeed, even the situation today is unsustainable. It is unsustainable in financial terms, without any question whatsoever. Major cost-cutting, improvements in productivity, and a certain drop in living standard in the short run will have to take place even if we encounter no political problems at all.

This adjustment will be much worse—and drastically so in most parts of the country—if we combine our financial problems with a political shock of the magnitude triggered by an affirmative Quebec referendum. In particular, the loss of ability of parts or the entire country to continue receiving net foreign cash infusions to sustain the standard of living will have its primary depressing effect and will then set off further internal declines in activity.

Uncertainty will continue for months or years in the absence of an accepted "Plan B." But even with such a plan, losses will be high and Quebec will be gone. With the best will in the world, we will all be poorer. With bad will, we will be much poorer, conceivably fighting each other economically and even militarily.

On the political front, ROC may fragment into several pieces. If that happens, the two western-most provinces will do well, Ontario will wallow in an aborted recovery and a diminished future, and the Atlantic will be devastated.

If ROC *does* find a way to stay in one piece, it will almost certainly be on the basis of a dramatically restructured central government (in Ottawa or wherever—there will be lots of extra space in Toronto or Calgary, too). This government will likely be more a service organization than anything else, existing primarily to deal with the deadweight of the federal debt and such minimal equalization as may still be affordable and agreed to by the richer provinces. The provinces will look after most of the government responsibilities at this point.

The central government will have little to do on the immigration front, because it will be all but stopped. Family reunification admissions, making up by far the bulk of our current intake, will be unaffordable. However, various parts of the country will still be looking for immigrants with both skills and money.

The customs and taxation units will be in business as usual; foreign aid will be non-existent; and external activities will be minimal. Embassies will be sold. The pensions of federal public servants and retirees of the poorer provinces and the Canada Pension Plan obligations will all be trimmed or reconsidered.

It is hard to say what will happen to the military—funds are always found for soldiers should the government need them. This cannot be foreseen.

There may or may not be a Parliament. Since the government will have virtually no discretionary revenue, there will be little reason for a Parliament. A Council of Ministers will better suit the needs of the paymasters, the three rich (or at least not bankrupt) provinces.

In short, what we call "Ottawa" will be but a shell of its former self. Cost sharing programs will be cut back to levels that the richer provinces will agree to, which will not be much.

Across the river, the new country of Quebec will be learning about the realities of debt and the cold world out there. There will be internal bickering, especially from the, say, 45 percent or more who voted against independence, as well as a lot of productivity loss and discomfort. Life will go on, but it will not be a pretty picture. And what is the greatest thing wrong with this picture? It is totally unnecessary.

Looking at this picture from the perspective of mid-1994, the temptation for most of us is to blame Quebec for having started all of this. There is an element of justice to this. Quebec will be the trigger.

But a trigger can only set off a loaded pistol. In this case, there must be a situation ready to explode. To illustrate this point, Vancouver Island could declare independence from British Columbia and life would go on pretty well unchanged. They are two healthy units, together or apart. Huge California could separate from the United States and it would make headlines, but not paupers. The United States government is deeply rooted and supported, and is financially viable. California would have its problems, but (curiously), freed of many of the Washington mandates that are so costly for it, the state would rapidly restructure its economy and social and migration policies to rekindle its prosperity. All of these entities are viable on their own; all have sufficient depth relative to their commitments to survive a shock.

The Quebec-ROC split does not have that depth. And the separation, if it comes, will come not from reasons of strength, but from reasons of weakness. The weakness in Quebec is that it feels sufficiently threatened to finally take the "beau risque" of René Lévesque (who used the words in the opposite federalist context) and go. It may be right or wrong, but when people roll dice that big, you have to believe they are motivated.

And as for ROC itself, it is suddenly revealed that the Emperor has no glue, so to speak. Once habit and inertia are jiggled, once every part of the country begins to question the usefulness of the centre, Ottawa, it turns out that some value it chiefly for cash (the Atlantic), some value it mainly to validate a commercial empire (Ontario), and some value it not at all (the West).[68]

So there we are. Quebec is indeed the trigger. And the loaded pistol is the "Ottawa system" of federation.

The comprehensive reasons for this split will be for historians to unearth from the enormous archaeological dig of the National Media Archive. The fact is we have arrived at a time when the pieces of Canada

---

68 Recall that we are talking here about Ottawa, not Canada. There is still today a huge affection for Canada in much of the country, and very little for Ottawa. *Ottawa is not Canada*—and Canada, as we know it, will be gone.

are ready to change. The old ways have brought most of us good lives at an unaffordable cost that we must now recognize and deal with. And our loyalties have been purchased by a centre that has run out of money.

Unless Quebec pulls the trigger, it now may be that the financiers will reduce our standard of living another way. The good thing about this path is that we would take our hits one at a time, and will temporarily avoid the costs of political change. However, if we are going to have to seriously rearrange our finances anyway, there is some argument for voluntarily making political changes at the same time, and doing so in a planned and orderly way.

For there is no doubt that the strains on the fabric of Canada require a restructuring whether Quebec forces it or not. If Quebec folds in the crunch as it may well do—there is nothing certain about the results of a referendum as of now—and if there is no fundamental change, in another decade the triggers to political change will be B.C. and Alberta. The financial changes will have long since happened.

Some readers will have a problem with this. Many will hope, and believe, that a referendum loss by the Parti Québécois will take us back to the good old days for which we elected Jean Chrétien in October 1993. But I don't believe it. The separatist sentiment exists in Quebec, stronger than ever, and it is not going away easily. Equally importantly, other parts of the country have grievances they want addressed. So things can be improved. And if you have come with me this far, journey yet a few pages more, to see what might be a better future. "Plan B" is the dreadful Ghost of Canada yet to Come, with every apology to Charles Dickens. "Plan C" is Scrooge reformed, Bob Cratchit happy, and Tiny Tim tossing his crutches and playing hopscotch on two legs.

Building "Plan C"

In building a "Plan C," which is designed not just to preserve Canada but also to make it better for everyone outside of Ottawa, one starts in two places. One is the unsatisfactory solution of an independent Quebec, and a hard or soft ROC, together or strung out. We shall have to build on that lowest denominator, and improve it.

The other place one starts with is the Ottawa of today, for whatever one thinks of how it does things, parts of what it does must be done by someone. The Ottawa government is made up of some 30 or so departments of government, depending upon how you count them, and around 95 boards, agencies and commissions. The Canadian Almanac, 1994, takes 42 pages to list them all.

An acceptable solution to everyone perhaps lies somewhere between these two starting points. To see what that solution might look like, let us ask the following questions:

1. What are the minimum things we might like a newly designed central agency[69] to do?

2. What add-ons to this minimum, if any, might we think are desirable?

3. Given the above, what kind of political control and financing rules might we want?

These questions can only truly be answered by a meeting of representatives of Canadians, be they members of governments or a Constituent Assembly. Nevertheless, it is worth making an attempt in advance to see if there is any range of hope.

In the area of "minimum requirements" of a central agency, one might list at least the following:

- a vehicle to preserve the "international personality" of Canada
- a vehicle to provide for full continuity of law as we pass from our current arrangements to those of the new structure.
- a vehicle to maintain, and even deepen, the Canadian common market
- a vehicle to perform the minimum collective or central service needs of the entities making up the new "Canada"

Let us consider these in turn.

---

69 I refrain from calling this a central *government* for the moment because it could be no more than a service agency, and we should not rule anything out at this stage.

International personality

The name "Canada" means something in the world. We are probably inclined to think we are more important than we really are, but "Canadian" is a useful label to sport as one travels around the world, and our participation in international agencies is somewhat enhanced by acting as one country. (Of course, if we were several, we would have more voices, and if they agreed, that would be effective too.)

So these aspects are useful. On balance, our membership in the G-7 and such organizations is far more important to the prime minister who attends and to the journalists who cover it than it is to ordinary folk, but there is some small merit in this. And Canada's peacekeeping activities have certainly been useful and appreciated by the world. That a restructured and more financially realistic Canada would be able to keep up these activities on the same scale, however, is extremely questionable— but it will be questionable anyway. We are broke in the sense of cutting out all non-essential expenditures, however we organize ourselves.

Much more important under this heading is the matter of international law and the continuity of all our current agreements on trade and other matters. This counts, and even if an independent Quebec and a fragmented ROC could put together a reasonable facsimile of the present arrangements after much negotiation, the waste of time and effort would be very costly. Moreover, the avoidance of the interim uncertainty would have quite a high value.

And what about the costs to the participants? Well, if Quebec (or any other of the entities) is absolutely determined to have its own embassies and seat in the United Nations, then it won't work. On the other hand, if the parts of the old Canada are prepared to share that UN seat, *and* the manner of instructing that vote, and share the operating costs of those embassies, then it could work. As to crass dollars, there would, of course, be large economies of scale in maintaining one international personality, and we will all need to think about money.

The final element of our international personality that is extremely important is the Canadian dollar. If we can find ways of preserving its integrity through common, planned, and orderly reform of our political structure, then we will avoid an immense amount of pain and turmoil, which would hit every one of us in the pocketbook.

Score this section a definite plus for some sort of "Plan C."

Continuity of law

In this book we have observed the numerous important legal questions that will have to be addressed in the breakup of a country, even if it will be just Quebec that goes. The most important of these are commercial questions of trade law, enforcement of judgements, property questions, trademarks and intellectual property, and the whole panoply of legal means of living together that we have worked out over 127 years. These are dull, even unknown to most of us. But they also comprise the underpinnings that make our system work, and making new arrangements will be costly, will add to uncertainty, and will enrich lawyers immensely which most Canadians will surely *not* see as an added advantage.

In addition, however, we are talking about a lot more than commercial law. The true flashpoints, the huge dangers of this independence and splitting exercise, if it unfolds, relate to international law and constitutional law. To take the two main examples, no one will be talking about the use of force in any context whatsoever if all our new arrangements come about under a continuity of law. And no foreign country will be talking about abrogating international agreements or denying accession to any part of Canada if we have continuity of law.

A "Plan C" which provides a legal, ongoing central organization for the parts of the old Canada, however weak that organization might be, would provide this essential element of continuity. What is important here is not which governments make the law on any given day, but that the legal framework continues and everything is done in that context.

Nevertheless, radical changes in the central organization would require constitutional amendments, which governments say they don't even want to talk about. This is temporary foolishness, in which they seek to avoid reality. They will talk.

Common Market

This section will need little justification for most readers, but it must be mentioned, for it cannot be assumed if the country breaks up.

Virtually everyone from the left to the right on the political spectrum, from the hardest separatist to the strongest federalist, pays at least lip service to the concept of maintaining a common market. Of course that does not get rid of barriers like marketing boards, even in present-day Canada, but we can take the principle as a given.

But as Patrick Grady says of a customs union in his survey, "It would be highly unrealistic to expect it to persist if political ties between Quebec and Canada were ruptured. . . . There can be no economic union without a political union."[70]

Minimum collective or central service needs

There are some things which it is better that a central service organization does. Passports and immigration are obvious examples. This section will review those areas.

(Please note: the fact that a central service organization performs certain duties says nothing about how the policies for performing those duties may be set. They could be set by an elected Parliament more or less as we have now; they could equally be set by agreement among the provinces that comprise the group using and supporting the central organization. This is the political as opposed to functional question, to which we shall return.)

In Chapter 8 we proposed a list of functions for a central agency. A bit of expansion is in order.

Security and defence

This function is an important economy-of-scale item, and it would be highly desirable to perform it in a collective and lower-cost way.

(Note here that "security" would normally be restricted to security *vis-à-vis* foreign interests. It is already the practice in Canada for internal security to be done by provincial governments, even though the RCMP is often the contractor for this purpose.)

---

70 *The Economic Consequences of Quebec Sovereignty*, The Fraser Institute, 1991.

Customs and immigration

The principle of maintaining a common market means that there is no need for customs points between provinces, but a new Canada, like the old, would have a continuing need for border controls on goods and persons. It would be more effectively done by a central group.

Debt management

One of the major problems of an independent Quebec and ROC in any configuration would, as we have discussed at some length, be the management of international debt, as well as access to any possible new or even rollover credit. But the problem is not universal. To put it bluntly, Ontario, B.C. and Alberta would come out way ahead, based on a scheme whereby each province assumed its share of the federal debt and only that. Any continued scheme whereby a central agency retained responsibility for the federal debt would, in effect, continue to involve the stronger provinces in a joint guarantee to benefit the weaker provinces, and also obligate them to continue to pay much more than their per capita share of a grotesquely enormous debt contracted in disproportionate part on behalf of the poorer provinces. In short, the negotiations around this issue might be tough.

At the end of the day (and overlooking any sentiment or generosity that the richer provinces would almost certainly bring to the table), the richer provinces would probably settle for a deal requiring them to pay more for the federal debt, in exchange for a veto over any increase in the debt and a gradual off-loading onto the several provinces as the longer-term bonds gradually matured.

In short, there are advantages to the collective in central debt management, which brings simultaneous *disadvantages* to the stronger players. Their price will almost certainly be a demand for increased control.

Note as well—and this is extremely important—that the above does not deal with the enormous contingent liabilities of the federal government. One cannot say from today's perspective how the negotiators of tomorrow will regard liabilities for publics service pensions, the Canada Pension Plan, various loan guarantees, and cost sharing plans. One can be virtually certain that there will be very considerable trimming.

The sum of these liabilities is a big number. According to a recent Fraser Institute study, these contingent and unfunded liabilities approximate $650 billion.[71] Yes, that was indeed *$650 billion*. The number is so enormous that it will have to be dealt with now in any major restructuring, rather than later as everyone has no doubt hoped.

Currency

A continuation of the Canadian dollar would be very highly desirable. Some entities—B.C. and Alberta, for instance—could get along perfectly well using the United States dollar, and, in due course, so could everyone, but the transition would be disruptive. There is no question that the continuation of the Bank of Canada on some basis would be a plus for everyone. Of course, the governing body would have to be changed to accommodate the provinces.

External relations

This issue is self-explanatory. Canada will become rather less proactive in the world due to financial strictures, whatever happens, but Canadians will still have international interests and will still need some kind of diplomatic and trade service to look after them. Again, the economies of scale are not only attractive, but almost obligatory if the job is to be done adequately.

Given the propensity of many of the provinces to establish their own foreign representative offices, one may be quite certain that the governance of the central diplomatic and trade function would reside with the provinces. (This would also be one way to deal in considerable part with the longing in some provinces for embassies of their own.)

Monitoring of inter-provincial/inter-regional agreements and rules

This would essentially be a secretariat function.

---

71   *Inside Canada's Government Debt Problem and the Way Out*, The Fraser Institute, 1994.

Inter-regional income transfers as agreed to by the parties

This would be the future equivalent of equalization. One may be quite certain that under a new arrangement to restructure the country, such transfer payments would be smaller, conditional (i.e., performance-based), and subject to the vetoes of the contributing provinces.

Weights, measures, and other such standards

This would be a low cost, obvious area for cooperation.

Necessary legal, tax, and administrative machinery to accomplish the above

Now in summary on this section, the above functions certainly do not comprise what most Canadians today think of as a country. On the other hand, two very positive things may be said about it:

- it is arguably better than the alternative, summarized at the beginning of this chapter, and,
- each area of cooperation is obviously mutually advantageous in its own right, as long as acceptable governing and decision-making machinery can be agreed upon.

Before looking at that, let us consider what central duties and responsibilities might notionally be added to the above minimum set.

Desirable add-ons to the central duties

There are a number of other things that a central government or service agency could usefully do in the Canadian circumstance. The extent to which any recombined group of provincial entities might be prepared to go along with this arrangement would depend, of course, on how the shots were being called. As a general proposition, the more regional control is provided, the more regions will be prepared to see a central agency do things on their collective behalf.

Major examples of this lie in the large fields of transportation, communications, and the environment. These are intrinsically overlapping jurisdictions, where there is some logic for centralized regulation. On the other hand, especially with respect to transportation and the environment, the provinces can handle more than they do today. And in communications, the major pre-occupation of the provinces tends to be software (program content) rather than hardware, though they would love to control those lucrative licenses allowing wires and air-waves to carry messages. If there is to be any cooperation in these matters, things will be worked out in the negotiations. Life will go on either way.

It is most unlikely that there will be any interest whatsoever in any central involvement in such matters as forestry, tourism, housing, lab-our, health, culture (multi- and otherwise), education, manpower, or social services. More precisely, the poorer provinces will have an interest in central involvement, but the controlling ones won't. The fisheries on the two coasts would presumably be controlled by the coastal provinces.

The matter of responsibility—if any—for aboriginal affairs is an important one. If we are to preserve the principle of continuity of law, this matter will have to be dealt with. (Under other scenarios, one suspects it would simply fall off the table in some parts of the country, though not in Quebec because it is too much of an issue *vis-à-vis* ROC.)

But it cannot be assumed that the old approach of the government of Canada in these matters would be continued. In any event, that approach has been so discredited it will have no mourners. The general issue, however, will surely receive much attention and emotion under any scenario.

All of the above issues would be matters for negotiation among the participating provinces under some kind of "Plan C," and it would be presumptuous to forecast results. However, there are a couple of areas where cooperation through a central agency would have such great advantages that it might be worth noting them at this point. The two concepts are *performance monitoring* and the *dissemination of ideas*.

One of the major criticisms that can be, and is, levelled at our existing federal setup is the degree to which Ottawa attempts to impose its views across the land. It does this through a combination of jurisdiction invasion in overlapping areas and financial muscle in cost-sharing areas. As the only entity with the right to tax across the country and pay out where it likes, it obviously has a lot of muscle. In any major restructuring, we may expect these tools and tendencies to disappear.

But this does not mean that Canadians living in different parts of the country do not have much to learn from each other. A central agency could do much to facilitate this. The key is the provision of a superb product by the centre, to be accepted on a voluntary basis by the provinces.

To make this explicit, let us look at education. There has long been a desirable role for a central measurement agency in Canada, but it has been absolutely impossible because of jurisdictional sensitivities. The provinces control education, and they are not about to let Ottawa get the tiniest part of its nose into the tent, as it has done in health and social services.

The appropriate role for the centre has nothing to do with authority or funding or the distortion of provincial priorities. But we do need in Canada a good deal more educational measurement, and there is a widespread consensus on this. This is the *performance monitoring* aspect, which is always uncomfortable for agencies that deliver programs, and is always good for their customers. There are significant variations between provinces in the way they run their education systems and the successes and failures they have. They prefer to not measure such things, and to keep them quiet when they do. But the public would be better served if some well publicized auditing were part of the picture. It would provide no authority—just the numbers.

And what about the "dissemination of ideas"? Once again, education will serve as an example. As our society becomes more and more complex, new methods are needed, and new methods are being found all over the world to come to grips with the challenges of education: dropouts, gifted kids, the variously challenged, streaming, et cetera. A central Office of Educational Research would be a good thing for the monitoring and pan-Canada diffusion of world results, as well as selected research of our own. Again, this would not be a big deal—there would be no programs to manage, no orders to issue. But the sharing and cross-fertilization of ideas is, in fact, the hallmark of human progress.

These two concepts, performance monitoring and the dissemination of ideas, could span the range of governmental activity, from social services to infrastructure, from administration to the environment. The key is simple. The local people run the show, absolutely. A mutually agreeable jury of professional peers gives advice and comment. If there is discrepancy, the customers—which means us—can decide.

Governance and financing of the central agency

With the easy part behind us—determining the minimum duties and the desirable add-ons—we now tackle the tough question. If we are to put together a new central agency or government for a restructured Canada, for a "Plan C," how are we to make the decisions in a way that most will think fair? And how will we find the funds in a way that most will agree to pay? This is the essential political question that must be resolved. We do have some guideposts.

There are two polar models. One is the European Union, where the individuals states run the show through a Council of Ministers. The other is the United States, where the centre easily has the lion's share of the clout. The present Canada is somewhere in between. (So are the federal states of Switzerland and Germany. The former in particular gives major powers to the Cantons, and, most unusually, to the people through a highly-developed system of direct democracy: referenda, et cetera.) In the circumstances it is very likely that the restructured Canada would have to be closer to the EU, but exactly how?

During the ill-fated period leading up to the last constitutional round, then-Minister Joe Clark commissioned a series of papers. They were invariably self-serving for the federal cause, but some were rather good nonetheless. One of these was "The European Community: A Political Model for Canada?" by Peter M. Leslie of Queen's University.[72] Leslie summarizes the most important lessons of the European Union for our country, and, in passing, makes the very important point that many who hanker for such an arrangement, especially those in Quebec, do not clearly understand that the EU model brings about new constraints as well as new freedoms. Yes, member states do indeed get to vote together on a range of government matters under the EU, but once

---

72   Ministry of Supply and Services Canada, 1991.

the vote is taken, they must abide by that decision. In the Canadian context, that would be tantamount to agreeing to have a collection of provinces override another province's decisions in, say, education.

Leslie also makes the very important point that it may be much harder for the centre to get things done in what he calls a *confederal* system.[73] Many of the things we have done through accommodation by elites at the federal level would have been a lot tougher to do at a federal-provincial conference. For example, he says that "in Canada it is unlikely that, under a confederal system, the Official Languages Act could have been passed; that a system of supply management for dairy products could have been introduced or could now be sustained, or perhaps that the present program of fiscal equalization could have been put in place." Like him, I leave readers to make up their minds as to whether this would be good or bad, whether it should be necessary to develop a true regional consensus by confederalism rather than by elite accommodation through our federalism in such things. The point is the system adopted makes a difference—a *big* difference.

The purpose of this chapter is not to present a full review of the above or any other work on this subject, but rather to point out the range of options. At one end of the spectrum is something rather like what we have today, fine-tuned in various ways to shift a power here, change a central institution there (a Triple-E senate, for example), and perhaps become a little more adventurous in decentralization and so-called "co-decision" where provinces are given more concurrent powers and more voice in federal policy-making.

At the other end of the spectrum is the confederal model wherein the ten states—provinces in our case—agree to act together to do certain things in common, for mutual benefit. The list presented earlier in this chapter gave a minimum target and some areas for expansion. The chief governing body in this sort of model is a Council of Ministers, requiring representation from each province, recording votes on each decision according to weighting rules (where population would be one compo-

---

73   In this system, member states control the centre through some system of weighted voting and financing, rather than having control by a Parliament directly elected by the people, with its own money and its own initiative.

nent, for example), which would attempt to recognize the interest of each state in any given subject. The weights could always be the same to prevent confusion, or they could vary for, say, financial questions to recognize that some pay more than others.

The important thing is that the initiating actors here would be provinces. They would govern a central bureaucracy that carries out the policies they consider to be mutually advantageous. Note that this model tends towards decentralization, but it can also lead to great central control in some areas, if the member states so agree under the weighted voting rules. The above case of invasion of exclusive decision-making in the field of education is only one example.

A confederal system can have a Parliament, as does the European Union. This Parliament is weak and mostly advisory, and this is typical of confederal systems. As a bow to confirmed federalists, even a weak Parliament can be represented as an institution that can grow in the fullness of time if the people so wish.

As well, the issue of a Parliament at the centre is a rather interesting barometer of our actual intentions. A central Parliament with real initiative is an appropriate instrument for a people who wish to do things together—a people who have an agenda, visions, and mutual goals that require proactive efforts by a centre that is larger than the constituent states. On the other hand, if our agendas, visions, and mutual goals as Canadians can be largely achieved in our own provinces, with the help of a central service organization, then a completely different structure is required.

It will not be for this book to opine as to which position in this option spectrum would best describe a government for Canada in the year 2000. But it is very possible to conclude this: for most Canadians, any of the above variations of "Plan C" would be preferable to an independent Quebec and a "Plan B" ROC.

But, if there is going to be any change, if it is going to be forced by the electorate of Quebec, then an "independent Quebec/'Plan B'/ROC" scenario is very likely where we are headed now. How do we get out of that trap, and into a positive quest for "Plan C"?

Getting there

Three broad arrays of forces can start us on a "Plan C" path. In order of least to greatest difficulty, those forces are the federal government, some combination of provincial governments, and some combination of ordinary citizens. Let us take these in turn.

In theory, the federal government could just "do it": state that the world is changing and that the whole arrangement of Canada is up for discussion, and then convene a believable and effective conference or assembly to do just that. This is extremely unlikely.

One impediment is the mindset of the government. It has a view of Canada that it is much like it should be at the present, and it doesn't want it changed. This is in no way a criticism. It is a statement of honourable belief, on which the government has been totally open and honest. It is difficult to see it calling for a dramatic re-examination of Canada.

Another impediment is public opinion. Most Canadians outside of Quebec would today find this a very far-fetched idea. They don't want to believe a referendum will pass, and they don't want to think about fundamental change. This is true today. However, as we have seen, public opinion can change far faster than governments can, as new realities sink in.

The third impediment is that even if such a process were triggered today by Ottawa, it might not only be thought incredible by most Canadians, but it might also be thought *unbelievable* by Quebeckers. After all, as the separatists never tire of repeating, they have heard all of these promises before, in 1982, in Meech, and in Charlottetown. Nothing has changed, they will say. This is another ploy: "Why should we waste our time?"

The bottom line is this: a federally sponsored rearrangement of Canada before a referendum is unlikely.

After a successful referendum, this will become a very different matter. The existing federal government, or a new one formed after an election called for that purpose, will have to confront a new and clear reality. The government of Quebec will have received its mandate for independence. The train will be on the track.

Serious federal action on constitutional change will become much more likely at this point. Unhappily, it will also have become much less acceptable to Quebec—certainly to the government of Quebec with a referendum mandate in its pocket and visions of embassies and a seat at the United Nations, and perhaps even to the people of Quebec, who, having gone through a huge trauma, might understandably consider such an idea too little, too late.

That doesn't mean that extremely vigorous action by Ottawa and ROC could not change this perception. If a people can be convinced that there is a seriously better idea out there, and that the alternative to looking at it will be a lot of pain, they will change. But it will not be easy, and the bona fides of Ottawa and the other provinces will be viewed with enormous scepticism.

The best we might be able to achieve would be a conditional view of events, a suspension of activity for a time, and a provision for Quebec observers at a Constituent Assembly. This would be a whole lot better than nothing, and it is our best shot. But it depends on an Ottawa that may or may not be able to come to grips with reality.

The second set of forces that might do something is the provinces. At first blush, this is laughable. They are not used to acting with genuine cooperation on serious matters, and indeed, they can seldom agree on the time of day in a room with only one clock. However, if and when these events unfold, most of the premiers will conclude at some point that this is an extremely serious business which affects their essential interests, and poses a major threat to the well-being of their residents. The wiser ones will also see an opportunity to fashion a better country. There may emerge a constitutional leader—a Clyde Wells of the day, so to speak—who will be able to mobilize his or her colleagues.

The provinces themselves could structure a Constituent Assembly. It would have no more legality than would a Quebec separation declaration; and even after approval in a province-by-province election, it would have no more constitutional force than would a Quebec referendum. But these are political questions and they will be determined by political will. The premiers, acting together, or mostly so, could begin a renewal process that, properly designed, could gain the confidence not just of their voters, but also of the entire country. May some bureaucrats in some provincial capital be working on such a plan right now! They have been quiet about it, if so. But it could work. We may have to take long shots.

And if our provincial government fails us as well? I have not the slightest doubt that citizen movements will appear, converse, amalgamate, grow, lobby, and, *in extremis*, try to form an Assembly themselves. This is the longest of long shots, and we cannot rely on it, or indeed, on any of the above.

For the fact is, that if a Quebec referendum passes, the "independent Quebec/'Plan B' ROC" scenario will be the most likely resolution of our conflicts. We could do much better, but events will be in the saddle, and the inertia that has bound us for so long will be our enemy as we try to change.

But there is hope. That is why one writes a book.

Epilogue

IT IS HARDER TO WRITE FUTURE HISTORY than past. The past has the common decency to sit still while outlines are drawn, details are studied, and facts filled in to sharpen the view. The future is shadowy, and blurred in its nature, a changeling whose real nature can never be known until it is captured by the moment.

Since this book was written, new polls have emerged, western premiers have issued warnings to Quebec, federalists have alternately told us to cool it on the one hand and to start talking straight on the other, and separatists have elucidated theories, old and new, to meet each new challenge.

And the world has continued to turn. That is about the only certainty. This outline of future history, like any other, is a rough and conditional thing. A principal actor may be hit by a truck, a financial or natural disaster may occur, and things may turn in a totally unexpected way.

Still, there are great currents in the affairs of humankind, and we have identified some of them here. The search for meaning and identity and material comfort and security by all people is eternal. The methods of achievement ebb and flow as our civilization matures.

In our time, transportation and communications have hugely expanded the world in ways that directly affect each of us, and knowledge and productivity have expanded our resources. We have responded in two ways. In a humanistic sense, we celebrate the worth of the individual. In a collective sense, we tend to place more importance on our smaller associations that provide protection and support in the great world around us.

This trend is as evident in Canada as it is elsewhere. It is shaping our lives and will continue to do so. The details will be very challenging, but our task is to set the course that accommodates the good of the new, while preserving the best of the old. Progress and preservation will always contend, as they contend in the Canada of today. Our job is to carefully understand and manage that meeting of forces, drawing the best from both.

Future history can be changed. Change for the better requires future thought. If this book inspires a bit of that, it will have served its purpose, however that history unfolds.

Appendix I: "Saying No"—Refusing to Negotiate and UDI

WHAT IF CANADA, AS REPRESENTED by the statements of Ottawa, simply refused to negotiate with a Quebec government that had obtained a majority referendum in favour of separation? What would be the consequences? Recall that in 1867, after the Confederation of Canada had been agreed to and the British North America Act passed in London, the Legislature of Nova Scotia voted not to join Canada. Indeed, in elections in September of 1867, 36 of 38 members of the Legislature and 18 of 19 members elected to the Ottawa Parliament explicitly opposed Confederation.

Nobody paid any attention to them, and the British law prevailed. Of course, everyone in the colonies in those days was used to obeying British law, so perhaps the Legislature never had a chance. By 1869, Nova Scotia leader Sir Joseph Howe had joined the federal cabinet in exchange for higher subsidies for his province, and the battle was over.

Could Ottawa ignore the Quebec Legislature, particularly if it were to act on a popular referendum rather than on its own account, as occurred in Nova Scotia? Well, that depends.

Take the toughest case for Quebec, as follows. Assume the referendum passes by a very narrow margin—just a shade over 50 percent—and that there are clear pockets of massive objection in West Montreal, the north, and perhaps one or two other areas. Assume further that there are indications out of Quebec that a significant percentage of the population will not support unilateral action by the Quebec government, but indeed will actively oppose it, by economic means, demonstrations, major firms' threats to move out of the province, and so on. Assume that this is accompanied by strong adverse signals from the financial community, most importantly a major sell-off of Quebec bonds and a temporary inability to raise new funds in Canadian or international markets.

What would happen then if Ottawa said something like this: "In something so basic as separation, there must be an overwhelming popular support. We will talk to you if and when you can demonstrate 60 percent support, and not before." Would Canada simply continue?

The Quebec government would be in a difficult spot. It could try a Unilateral Declaration of Independence (UDI), and we will discuss that below. But its more likely response would be to express moral outrage, work to encourage anti-Ottawa sentiment among Quebeckers to try to make the pro-independence numbers grow, and declare a moratorium on further separation activity in order to reassure financial markets that the rule of law would prevail. In the meantime, the Bloc Québécois MPs in Ottawa would go about their business in tying Ottawa in knots, as foreshadowed by Leader of the Opposition Lucien Bouchard in May of 1994.[74]

The book on this whole strategic approach was effectively written by the separatists of the Irish Free State in the early part of this century. Between occasional rebellion and continued destabilization in the home territory and extremely annoying action in Parliament, they gradually wore down the British authorities, who capitulated in 1921 and granted independence.

Such a long and costly war of attrition could not appeal to anyone. Unlike the Irish question, when the British Empire bestrode the world and when an annoyance in a small province, even one close to home, was not important overall, a separation of Quebec cuts to the core of Canada. One cannot treat it as a mere annoyance, as the British could

---

74   Canadian Press reports, May 31.

consider Ireland, because the Canadian example would destroy certainty and the ability to plan.

As we have noted before, uncertainty is the enemy of getting on with our lives and all it entails: investment, careers, retirement planning, home purchases and sales, the future of our children, and the very basics of our lives. The conclusion: if such a war of attrition could be sustained by Quebec for just a few years, the separatists would get their wish. It might take one more federal and one more provincial election, either of which could be fatal to the separatist cause. But if they won both, they would win their prize.

But that is not all. The cost to *all* of us would be vastly raised by the exercise, no matter who won. The very fundamental costs of uncertainty raised in the last paragraph need not even be quantified for that point to be clear.

If either side does not like this idea, there are two ways out. One is the Czechoslovak solution of the larger party saying in effect, "If you want to go, we don't even want to examine the bona fides very closely. Just go quickly!" And they did. No referendum was held in either of the two parts of the country. After the election of two strong governments in 1992, each at what we would call a "provincial" level in the soon-to-be Czech and Slovak Republics, the deal was simply done, though it was clear from opinion polls that the two publics supported this. That is the easy way out, if both sides agree.

And what happens if both sides don't agree, and one wants to go ahead *now*, rather than fight the above-mentioned war of attrition? That is when you get a Unilateral Declaration of Independence. It may or may not work. A Quebec government will not be ignorant of the following factors, which may in part guide their thinking.

1. The act of a UDI is not a legal process. It is a *political* one. It is not something done according to law, unless the "natural law" invoked in the United States Declaration of Independence is what one means by the word. There is only one law governing UDI, and that is the law of survival. If you survive, you win. If you don't, you lose.

2. The true jury that must accept or reject a UDI is not, as is commonly thought, the international community. This is a har-

dened group that talks much about morality, but in fact accepts reality, be it a Saddam Hussein (when he was a pal) or the nuclear weapons-producing North Korea, within very broad limits of tolerance. Any conceivable new government of Quebec that can persuasively control its own territory would be well within the limits of a state that the international community would be prepared to deal with, after some minimum decent interval, which would not be long.

3. The true jury is purely and simply the population of Quebec. This is also the *toughest* jury, and the greatest worry for any separatist government that would contemplate a UDI, for a successful UDI requires quite massive citizen support, in a modern technological state. That is the true test that must be passed.

The theory

To digress briefly into theory, a UDI will be successful if and only if it satisfies the following conditions:

a) The secessionist government has a solid control of its territory, and is capable of standing firm against enemies from within.

b) The military forces of the secessionist government are superior to any force that may be deployed against them.

c) The economics work.

To illustrate, the all-time champion UDI was, and remains, the American Revolution. In 1776, a delegate of the State of Virginia laid before the Congress a resolution that "these United Colonies are, and of right ought to be, free and independent States, and that they are absolved from all allegiance to the British Crown, and that all connection between them and the State of Great Britain is, and ought to be, totally dissolved." A committee was appointed consisting of Thomas Jefferson, John Adams, Benjamin Franklin, Roger Sherman, and Robert Livingston, which concluded with Jefferson's draft of the Declaration of Independence. The government controlled the territory. Moreover, it reflected the spirit of the people.

During the War of Independence, the military forces of the secessionist government were superior to the British troops sent to fight against them. The appetite for major military deployment was limited in Britain, though it was still a far stronger military power at the time.

And . . . the economics worked. Did they ever!

The all time champion *war* of UDI happened in that same vigorous country, after the secession of the South. The first and third conditions worked (loyalty and economics); the military survivability condition didn't.

More recently, the secession of the state of Biafra from Nigeria in 1969 did not work due to a mixture of military and economic pressures. The UDI of the Rhodesia remnant of Sir Roy Wellensky's Rhodesian Federation, under Ian Smith, lasted for quite a time, until it was brought to its knees by a combination of economics and lack of popular support, for, of course, this government spoke only for the small white minority. Even so, it lasted for a surprising length of time against very determined international economic sanctions, shored up by clever blockade evasions and the total loyalty of the local white establishment.

The most recent set of UDI candidates has mostly been successful, in the wake of the disintegration of the former Soviet Union. Numerous former republics-in-name-only issued UDI proclamations—and made them stick! Curiously, this happened in defiance of the third principle, namely that the economics ought to work. They didn't, but since they hadn't under the old arrangement either, it didn't seem to matter. This incredible dissolution of a major empire gone soft at the core in a matter of weeks is one of the remarkable phenomena of history.

And Quebec?

The UDI route for Quebec almost certainly satisfies two out of three conditions. The economics are very tough, but they will work at a lowered standard of living. The prospect of having to repel outside military force seems remote. This is more a matter of will in ROC than anything else, for surely even our limited Canadian Forces, counting only those based outside of Quebec, could fairly quickly occupy the basic set of government offices, television stations, and those few other places that are needful in such circumstances. To even write of it is so un-Canadian. It seems very unlikely.

But satisfying the first principle that the local government has a solid control of its territory—ah!—now there is another story.

Consider what a successful UDI means. When the smoke clears, it begs the question, will the citizens pay taxes and obey the law? We live in a society where such things are mostly self-policing, done voluntarily. They can also be compelled by a police state, but that simply would not work in any part of Canada in this day and age, short of a massive repressive apparatus imported from somewhere else, which one cannot foresee. So citizen cooperation is required.

To be specific, it is required in the areas of:

- paying taxes—to Quebec City now, not Ottawa. Needless to say, the Ottawa compliance mechanisms will be gone. (On the other side, Quebec has its own income tax enforcement capability.)

- obeying the law. There are a million things that we collectively do every day to make our society work. If half a million of us stopped obeying the law in targeted ways, we couldn't be put in jail—and in fact, no one would ever know, for most offences, from not buying dog licenses, to sending in false statistical data (required for compliance), to an anglophone merchant defiantly putting up an English sign to see what happens. A widespread pattern of civil disobedience of all the smaller laws will destroy any democratic government.

- working with others. This is the ultimate sanction. An independent Quebec, whether born of UDI or otherwise, must profit by the released energy of its people in order to succeed, and must overcome the additional transitional costs of the new status as well as the long term costs of the larger debt. This means working together, effectively. This requires enthusiasm. It cannot be compelled.

But what if the referendum vote is only a bit over 50 percent?

Precisely! In other words, the massive degree of voluntarism required to achieve a successful UDI in our affluent, democratic North American context is very unlikely to be forthcoming. The "No!" voters are not going to help achieve the "Yes!" voters' agenda, because most of them won't agree with the separatist plan any more after the vote than they did before. That is one of the ways a referendum on such absolute basics as changing countries differs from one on, say, whether we should adopt the metric system. On the latter, if I lose, I sigh and measure in metres tomorrow, with reasonable good will. On the separation question if I lose—well, I may not, probably won't, cooperate.

My conclusion is that a Quebec UDI would not work.

And as always, there is a caveat. If the tactics of either Ottawa or ROC were of a nature to polarize and unite Quebeckers of all views during this process, matters could change overnight. Random acts of foolishness if grouped together in time—a flag-burning incident, a beating of Quebec tourists somewhere in ROC, intemperate politicians—can cause unforeseeable things to happen.

Remember, the only element of UDI lacking for Quebec is massive popular support. It would be irrational to do things to supply this missing element. If ROC wants to split from Quebec, there are less costly ways of doing it.

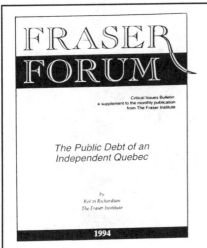

The New Federalist

By
Gordon Tullock

$19.95 paperback
141 pages; ©1994
ISBN 0-88975-164-1

How can government become more efficient?

The answer, world-renowned economist Gordon Tullock explains, is to let governments compete with each other. Governments that remain inefficient will lose their tax base and be forced to mend their ways. Tullock masterfully explains how Canada could move toward such a system and the benefits Canadians would recieve.

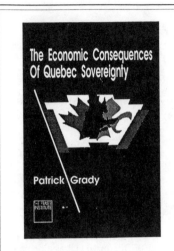

The Economic Consequences of Quebec Sovereignty

by
Patrick Grady

$19.95 paperback
184 pages
1991
ISBN 0-88975-137-4

Quebeckers have been lulled into a false state of complacency about their economic future by the reassuring voice of the Bélanger-Campeau Commission. This book seeks to inform Quebec and the rest of Canada about the economic disruption that would be unleashed if failure to accommodate Quebec's legitimate demands causes Quebec to opt out of Canada.

The book's main conclusion is that the costs of separation would be very high for Quebec. While the costs would be lower for the rest of Canada, they would still be significant. Indeed, if Quebec were to separate and relations between Canada and Quebec were to become acrimonious, the consequences could be economically disastrous for everyone.

Will Canada Survive?

Edited by
A.R. Riggs and Tom Velk

Federalism in Peril:

National Unity,
Individualism, Free Markets, and
the Emerging Global Economy

edited by
A.R. Riggs and Tom Velk

$19.95 paperback
204 pages; 1992
ISBN 0-88975-141-2

How did Canada, land of "peace, order and good government," arrive at a constitutional crisis that imperials its existence as a nation? Have Ottawa's options narrowed to drastic decentralization, a mere economic union, or breakup? If not, what concessions should be offered to Quebec to keep the country intact?

These and other questions are here addressed in a series of 20 papers by leading academics, journalists and experts on public policy issues. They include:

* The Right Honourable Pierre Elliott Trudeau on the importance of popular sovereignty and individual versus collective rights

* Stephen Scott on the legitimacy of force if breakup should occur

* Michael Walker on guarantees for private property and other essentials for an amendment package

Contributors also probe the economic costs of separation, discuss aboriginal accommodation, and isolate fundamental principles for defending and strengthening federalism.